# The United States and the PROMESA to Puerto Rico

# The United States and the PROMESA to Puerto Rico

## An Analysis of the Puerto Rico Oversight, Management, and Economic Stability Act

María de los Angeles Trigo

San Juan, Puerto Rico

For permissions and information contact:
América en Libros
info@americaenlibros.com

First Edition
Digital, August 2016
Print, June 2019
ISBN 978-0-9998088-1-8

Quotation on page 98 republished with permission of Harvard Law Review conveyed through Copyright Clearance Center, Inc.

Edited by Anabel Hernández, ahgtranslation@gmail.com
Book Layout ©2013 BookDesignTemplates.com
Cover Layout by Creativindie, www.creativindiecovers.com
Cover image used under license from Shutterstock.com
www.shutterstock.com/g/xtock

# Contents

*For my parents.*

*For believing "Why?" is always an appropriate question,*
*and that a little skepticism never hurt anyone.*

*We know that no one ever seizes power with the intention of relinquishing it. Power is not a means, it is an end.*

—GEORGE ORWELL
1984

# Preface

PUERTO RICO AND THE United States have a relationship that is difficult to define and classify, especially under international law.

Puerto Rico was ceded by Spain to the United States at the end of the 1898 Spanish-American War. The U.S. had been keen on taking control of Puerto Rico since its armed forces, particularly its Navy, considered Puerto Rico an important element in the new strategy for the expansion of the U.S.'s influence in the world.

Since the mid-1800s the U.S. had identified the military benefits of controlling Puerto Rico: a country almost equally distant from North and South America, and the first territory in the American continent reached from Europe when travelling west through the North Atlantic Ocean. Controlling Puerto Rico represented an unparalleled defensive and offensive military and commercial advantage to the U.S., a new country who saw itself as the heir of the European empires.

In the Paris Peace Treaty of 1898, Spain made provisions for the treatment that the Puerto Rico inhabitants would receive from their new metropolis — if they had been born in Spain. However, inhabitants of Puerto Rico born in Puerto Rico were reserved no rights: "The civil rights and political status of the native inhabitants of the territories hereby ceded to the United States shall be determined by the [U.S.] Congress."[1]

For over a century Puerto Ricans have been at the mercy of the U.S.'s military and commercial strategies, which have been aided by the special and expansive interpretations the U.S. Supreme Court has made of the Territorial Clause of the U.S. Constitution. Such interpretations have effectively granted plenary powers to the U.S. Congress over Puerto Rico, which it exercises through the Committee on Natural Resources of the House of Representatives, and the Committee on Energy and Natural Resources of the Senate.

As recently as a month ago, these interpretations based on nineteenth-century ideas of racial superiority and imperial aspirations were upheld by the U.S. Supreme Court.

Autonomy, self-government, sovereignty, and justice can be very flexible terms.

I am Puerto Rican. I have lived in Puerto Rico all my life. And since the U.S. invaded Puerto Rico in 1898 we have been subject to the decisions, and whims, of the U.S. Congress.

Legal interpretations of the Territorial Clause of the U.S. Constitution affect my rights and my life in a way that people living in the U.S. cannot comprehend.

And how could they? Puerto Rico is absent from the public discourse in the U.S. It is absent from the political discourse. Puerto Rico is invisible in the main media, and in most of the alternative media, too.

And that facilitates manipulating the U.S. population when Puerto Rico is the subject of discussion.

Very few books have been written about this relationship addressed to the reader who would like to know more about the ties that bind Puerto Rico to the U.S. without having to delve into academic treatises, historical volumes, or legal analyses.

I try to fill that void with this book regarding the U.S. Congress's response to Puerto Rico's economic crisis. A response that Congress tried to design in the face of electoral pressures; not only from voters, but also from rich and influential campaign donors.

I believe analyses about Puerto Rico must consider the historical background of its constitutional development, as well as its relationship with the U.S. Puerto Rico's legal framework, constitutional boundaries, and political realities and limits are unique — even if some features seem similar to those of sovereign states or U.S. states.

This will be the first book in a series that will discuss different aspects of this metropolis-colony relationship still playing out in the twenty-first century, told from the perspective of someone whose life is subject to foreign plenary powers that should have been abolished a long time ago.

And let me clarify: I aim to provide you with insights and information rooted in Puerto Rico's history, and its legal and political status, so you can better understand Puerto Rico's fiscal and legal structures, and economic constraints.

But I do not claim to be objective. I am a Puerto Rican, writing about Puerto Rico. My opinions are duly identified, but research does not whitewash history; it just puts today's actors, and actions, in context.

It is my hope that you will find this information useful, intriguing, and eye-opening.

Thank you for reading.

San Juan, Puerto Rico
July 2016

[–]

# Author's Note

I HAD FINISHED ANALYZING the bill at Chapter 8 of the book, convinced that it would die of inattention in the U.S. Congress. However, Congress surprised me on 18 May 2016 with a new version of the PROMESA.

That is why you will see in Chapter 8 an analysis debunking the precedent argument that the U.S. Congress finally dismissed quite forcefully in the summary to the bill's version of 18 May 2016. The reasons given echo my analysis.

Since it seemed the bill would go through Congress, I kept updating the analysis the same way I had written Parts 1 and 2: contemporaneously with new developments, so I could end up with a book that analyzed the bill's travails through Congress.

I decided to publish it after the enactment of the bill on 30 June 2016, when it was signed into Public Law 114-187.

Some chapters in Parts 1 and 2 were originally published in LinkedIn throughout March and April 2016 and have been edited and expanded for publication in this book.

The web pages referred to in the book were last accessed on 31 July 2016.

[0]

# Introduction

PUERTO RICO IS IN the midst of an economic, fiscal, and financial crisis not seen since the early twentieth century. Its economy has been contracting for over ten years, population has decreased for the first time in its history, it has high levels of unemployment, public debt has increased exponentially, government revenues have decreased, businesses have closed, and jobs have disappeared.

The Puerto Rico government has been increasing taxes to try to generate more government revenue while cutting expenditures.

How did we get here?

Puerto Rico does not have a diversified economy, in part because for decades it has concentrated its efforts on wooing foreign capital, mostly through tax incentives, to establish businesses in Puerto Rico. The strategy worked when Puerto Rico's labor force was relatively uneducated and labor costs were low. Plenty of U.S. companies arrived on Puerto Rico for the low-cost labor and the free trade with the U.S.

Puerto Rico's economic growth was also based on huge military investments made by the U.S. government on the run-up to Second World War. These included improvements in infrastructure, since Puerto Rico was an important bastion in the Allies' war strategy.

During the 1970s, in the midst of the oil crisis, Puerto Rico's economy started to falter and social unrest increased, particularly against the U.S. and its presence in Puerto Rico. The U.S. responded by increasing its repression of the independence movement, but also by enacting a tax credit program that would exempt from the federal corporate income tax the income that U.S. companies generated from their operations in Puerto Rico and other "possessions."

Section 936 of the U.S. Internal Revenue Code created a boom: plenty of new well-paid jobs, more cash in the economy, increased government revenues, and a high level of bank deposits that fueled credit concessions. But it was all based on the federal tax credit, and the Puerto Rico government did not do any long-term planning, nor implemented economic development or structural changes while the provision was in place.

Eventually the U.S. adopted the policy of promoting international free trade agreements, which not only eliminated the main competitive advantage Puerto Rico had, but also increased its disadvantages, since Puerto Rico still had to comply with all federal laws and regulations that increased the costs of doing business in Puerto Rico.

And then the U.S. signed the World Trade Organization agreement on subsidies, which prohibited tax programs like Section 936.

In none of these cases did the U.S. grandfather Puerto Rico, nor studied how its economy would be affected by the treaties. Neither has it authorized Puerto Rico the use of additional tools to make up for the competitive advantages that it has been losing.

At present, the U.S. is secretly negotiating trade treaties with Asia and Europe, and Puerto Rico cannot plan for the effects those treaties will have on its economic development strategy.

The world's economy is getting more interconnected, and Puerto Rico is out of the loop. Plenty of the constraints come from the U.S. Others, however, come from Puerto Rico's inability to plan for its future and to fight for its right to be a part of the community of nations.

So we arrive at the present-day situation: not enough jobs, less government revenues, less population, less taxpayers, and plenty of austerity that has contracted the economy even more.

At this juncture, the Puerto Rico government tried to negotiate its debt, since it soon would be out of money to pay it.

But the debt documents require that all creditors agree to the changes, which is practically impossible. Puerto Rico government entities could not file bankruptcy because the

U.S. Congress had inexplicably prohibited it. Puerto Rico needed a way to restructure its debt. So it enacted a law that would authorize some of its municipalities to do that.

But some creditors challenged the law in federal district court, arguing that Puerto Rico had no authority to restructure its debt. They argued that Puerto Rico had no choices but to: pay its debt; request the consent of all creditors; or ask the U.S. Congress for a solution, considering its plenary power over Puerto Rico.

The court agreed with the creditors, and the appeals court affirmed. The U.S. Supreme Court decided that it would review the case.

Meanwhile, Puerto Rico had been paying its debt as it came due, but in June 2015 the Governor of Puerto Rico stated that the debt was unpayable.

In August 2015 the Puerto Rico government partially defaulted on its debt for the first time in history. And even though it made payments due in October and December 2015, in January 2016 it defaulted in all the payments that were due.

That is when the PROMESA started.

# [PART 1]

## Versions of 24 and 29 March 2016

[1]

# The Promise to Put the Uppity Commonwealth in its Place

WHAT AN INAUSPICIOUS BEGINNING. The discussion draft issued by the Committee on Natural Resources of the monstrosity that is the Puerto Rico Oversight, Management, and Economic Stability Act[1] shows that the bill is just the PROMESA of the ever-present control over Puerto Rico through the ever-despotic territorial clause.

I will divide my comments on the U.S. PROMESA to Puerto Rico in this Part 1 into these themes:

- the Board's foundations put in place in the bill
- the insidious extraneous government being "incorporated" into Puerto Rico's government structure

- the process established in the bill for a possible restructuring of debt
- the reinstallation of the U.S.'s economic powers and political interest groups as the entities in control of Puerto Rico's assets and investments.

My comments refer to the draft issued on 29 March 2016. I may also refer to the language used in the draft of 24 March 2016,[2] depending on the changes made from one draft to the other.

## The Summary that Says It All

The Board is created to "assist" the Government of Puerto Rico in managing its public finances, audit the government, and address the financial crisis. The Committee's Legislative Summary clarifies that the Board will do so in "the most efficient and equitable manner that is respectful of the rule of law, self-governance and all involved parties and creditors."[3]

Forgive my skepticism.

The Board created is an "entity within" the government of Puerto Rico, but is not subject to any control, oversight or review from either the Governor or the Legislative Assembly. No explanations need be given as to anything the Board does.

I do not understand how that works. How can an entity be within the government of Puerto Rico, but not report to the constitutional head of the government, I do not understand.

Unless this entity is a supra-government: every financial decision made by the Governor or the Legislature must be approved by the Board, in its sole discretion, before it may come into effect. And, since public policies depend on moneys assigned, guess who will be establishing public policy in Puerto Rico?

The Board — you got that right.

On the other hand, those creditors that were "badly hurt" in the Detroit bankruptcy must be ecstatic.[4] Congress adopted their view of the unjustness of their suffering, and has declared that:

- following the 200-year precedent of the retro-activeness of bankruptcy is "ill conceived" and "would undermine the rule of law."[5]

For sure it would undermine the rule of the law as the U.S. Congress would like it to be, not as it is. See Chapter 8 for a brief discussion.

- prioritizing pensions over creditors "would also have serious consequences on the broader municipal bond market."[6] (Detroit again.)

Chapter 8 discusses the arguments presented by creditors when they complained to Congress that they had suffered much in Detroit's bankruptcy and they said that Puerto Rico had — had — to be different. I hand it to them: they are in the wrong in law and in equity, but boy do they indeed have the lobbyists.

## The Unvarnished Purpose

So this Board is an administrator of Puerto Rico's budget, with the priorities set by the U.S. President through the members he appoints.

Let us be real. The Board's purpose is to make sure the debt payments of the next few years are made, so that the creditors that skimped in due diligence can clear their positions and limit their losses.

Puerto Rico's economic development? ... What? What? I don't hear you.

This reminds me of the civil government "granted" to Puerto Rico by the Foraker Act of 1900, whose members (including the Supreme Court of Puerto Rico) were all appointed by the U.S. President.[7]

## First Things First

Nowhere in this bill is there any mention of economic recovery, economic activity, economic research, economic structure, economic development, economic limitations, or economic constraints. Not once do the powers of the Board mention anything remotely related to economic activity that would set the bases for higher government revenues.

The Board's powers specified in the bill concentrate on controlling expenses, constraining disbursements, and reducing the government.

And what happens after the Board's term? That is not the Board's problem. If the government is inoperative because of the financial squeeze? It is not the Board's problem. If the privatized services are not up to par? Not the Board's problem. If the economy contracted even more under the Board's stewardship? Not the Board's problem.

## The Steward of the U.S. Creditors

The first part of the bill sets the foundation for the Financial Oversight and Management Board, and all the actions that will be taken by its members. The bill's Title I also establishes the Board's powers, legal protections, and its unlimited discretion.

The Board will have five members appointed by the U.S. President, of which two must be selected from a list provided by the Speaker of the U.S. House of Representatives, and other two from a similar list provided from the Majority Leader of the U.S. Senate. The initial appointment is for three years. The President can remove them only for cause.

The list provided by the Speaker must include a person that either maintains a primary residence, or has a primary place of business, in Puerto Rico. The draft of 24 March required that two people meet this condition, but in that draft all five members were named by the President after consultation with the Committee on Natural Resources of the House, and the Committee on Energy and Natural Resources of the Senate.[8]

The only requirement for the Board's members is "knowledge and expertise in finance, management, law, or the organization or operation of business or government."[9]

> There is no requirement whatsoever for someone with some knowledge of economic development. Neither do they ask for some basic knowledge of Puerto Rico's government and economic structure, nor for an understanding of the legal constraints in its relationship to the U.S. Nothing of the sort seems to be necessary.

Another requirement is that no family member of the potential Board member be either an employee or a contractor of the Puerto Rico government. This will disqualify a lot of knowledgeable, competent people that could be willing to work with the Board. Is that the desired outcome?

> I find it very revealing that the bill does not prohibit conflict of interest of its members regarding present or future negotiations for the sale of goods and services to the Puerto Rico government.
>
> There is a placeholder for a prohibition on "any other conflict of interest,"[10] but the fact that it is still a placeholder is, by itself, remarkable.

## The Crackdown

Although the bill makes clear that the civil service laws of the federal government do not apply to the Board, it provides for the recruitment of federal employees, who may elect to be considered as federal employees while they are employed by the Board.

More interestingly, a person who is recruited by the Board may elect to be considered a federal employee for purposes of the Thrift Savings Plan, life insurance, and health insurance.

> I suppose this is considered a carrot to make it easier for the Board to recruit qualified personnel. Congress must know it will not be easy.

The most jarring provision of this bill (and the one who makes obvious the bill's intent) is the authorization that the "Board shall ensure the purposes of this Act are met including by prompt enforcement of the laws of Puerto Rico prohibiting public sector employees from participating in a strike or lock out."[11]

This prohibits dissent.

> After centuries of police and military repression, and decades of persecution by the FBI, such a blanket statement of "ensur[ing] the purposes of this Act are met" makes me expect a Board that will believe the ends justify any means.
>
> Awful times may be here again.

In that same vein: any officer or employee of the Puerto Rico government who intentionally provides to the Board information that is false or misleading shall be guilty of a misdemeanor and fined not more than $1,000.

> Note that this crime is reserved for officers or employees of the Puerto Rico government; it does not apply to any federal government employee providing services to the Board, nor to any employee recruited directly by the Board. It still makes my blood boil, even if this version eliminated the year of jail that was incorporated in the 24 March draft.[12]

The 24 March draft also provided for a Chief Management Officer that would have been responsible for the oversight and supervision of departments and functions of the Puerto Rico government.[13] The 29 March draft eliminated this position that was tasked with improving the effectiveness and efficiency of the Puerto Rico government.

## The Courts Where We Go

Any action related to the bill must be brought in the District Court for the District of Columbia, and any order may be appealed only to the Court of Appeals for the District of Columbia. Even more astounding, the term to petition for a review by the U.S. Supreme Court is reduced to 10 days (the normal term is 90 days).

Does this mean there is mistrust in the U.S. Congress towards the Puerto Rican judges sitting in the federal court in Puerto Rico? This bill is drafted for Puerto Rico, and all of its titles apply to Puerto Rico. Nevertheless, the legal actions must be brought before the federal court in the District of Columbia?

What is the purpose of requiring that any action related to the bill be brought in the District Court for the District of Columbia, and appealed only to the Court of Appeals for the District of Columbia? To make it more difficult and expensive for Puerto Rico and Puerto Ricans to litigate? So that if the U.S. Supreme Court held in Puerto Rico's favor in the two cases pending this term, Puerto Rico would think about challenging the territorial clause as the legal basis for this bill? And that if that were the case, it would be better for the U.S. if Puerto Rico had to argue before courts unfamiliar with its legal relationship with the U.S., and far away from San Juan?

Title III on Adjustment of Debts (discussed in Chapter 4) is the only title of the bill that applies to other jurisdictions, and the bill states that the federal court with venue for actions under that title is the district court for the territory that will restructure its debt under the title. So this exclusive jurisdiction in the District of Columbia courts was included to affect only Puerto Rico.

Importantly, the bill prohibits any injunctive relief against the Board that would take effect before all appeals have been taken or until the order is final. This means that a decision by a court prohibiting the Board to do something or ordering it to do something cannot take effect until no party has any other appeal to file.

## Me? Responsible?

Neither the Board nor its members or employees are liable for any claim against the Board, its members, its employees, or the Puerto Rico government that results from actions taken to carry out the PROMESA.

> Note that the bill does not exempt the Puerto Rico government or its employees from claims that result from the implementation of the bill, even though the bill makes it a misdemeanor to disobey an order from the Board!

The Puerto Rico government is not exempt from liability for following the orders of the Board.

> Does the U.S. Congress want to keep a pocket open, and it will be the Puerto Rico government?

## Who Pays

The Board will establish its own budget, and may make sure that its control over the budgetary process of the Puerto Rico government will grant it sufficient funds to operate at the level of expenses it deems necessary. Its budget is not subject to any kind of review, since the "annual expenses of the Oversight Board [are] as determined in the Oversight Board's sole and exclusive discretion."[14]

It sounds eerily familiar to that statement of "the standard of living to which it has become accustomed."

In addition, the Puerto Rico government must provide a "dedicated funding source"[15] that is not subject to subsequent legislative appropriations. I suppose the easiest thing would be to create a new revenue stream: a new tax that could be called the Board Imposed and Added Tax Stream, or BIATS.

That makes for an interesting acronym, doesn't it?

Now let me discuss an entertaining part of this Title I: the authorization granted to the Board to issue, in the name of Puerto Rico, bonds sufficient to fund the Board for at least five years. Congress will appropriate funds (the amount is still blank) so the Board can hire professionals to help it in the organization of the Board and the process of establishing a funding source.

Here you have it:

- Congress authorizes the Board to issue long-term debt for operational expenses, and
- appropriates funds for the hiring of financiers and consultants to issue such bonds.

## Wages Down Forever

The bill amends the U.S. Fair Labor Standards Act of 1938 to extend the age at which Puerto Rico employees may be subject to a minimum hourly wage of $4.25.

Normally, an employer may pay an employee who is younger than 20 years old a wage of $4.25 instead of $7.25 "during the first 90 consecutive calendar days after such employee is initially employed."[16] For Puerto Ricans exclusively, this bill increases the age to 25.[17]

> University graduates (of which Puerto Rico has a rate equivalent to the U.S.) usually finish their university degree when they are 21. With this amendment, recent graduates will be subject to the same depressed wage that applies to high school and university students.

But that is not all. The bill makes the depression on wages quite expansive for Puerto Rican employees by declaring that the regulations issued in 2015 by the U.S. Department of Labor updating the overtime regulations[18] do not apply and "shall have no force or effect" in Puerto Rico.[19]

> This regulation was issued to increase worker's income, which has a positive effect on government revenues and the economy.
>
> Through this amendment the U.S. Congress ensures that Puerto Rican workers will never benefit from such regulation, since the prohibition is indefinite. For such a regulation to apply, the U.S. Congress would have to enact a law amending the PROMESA to that effect.
>
> I would love to know who is advising the Members of Congress (I suppose someone is). If wages are

depressed, government revenues go down, sales and use tax revenues go down, consumption of electricity goes down. From where do the drafters of this bill think the money is going to come to pay the debt?

## Self-Determination

And in case you, like me, thought that we were back to 1900, the bill wants to remind us that "Nothing in this Act shall be interpreted to restrict Puerto Rico's rights to determine its future political status..."[20]

## Whose Interests?

The cards are clearly stacked in favor of creditors, for whose protection the Board was conceived. The tasks of the Board are to squeeze Puerto Ricans to provide for the payment of debt, and, more galling, to provide funding for the Board that will set its own "standard of living."

And so, the foundations have been laid for the interests and priorities of the U.S. government and the powerful lobbyist groups to take public center stage in the management of Puerto Rico resources.

[2]

# A Takeover Is a Takeover

THIS PROMESA IS GOING back to the future. It is the spiritual child of the Foraker Act of 1900 (which created the infamous civil government "granted" to Puerto Rico after two years of U.S. military rule).[1] A better name for this PROMESA would be Foraker 21. So analogous are the supra-government created by the Board to the Foraker Act's Governor appointed by the U.S. President and the Executive Council appointed by the U.S. President (and the hobbled Puerto Rico government to the hobbled Foraker Act's House of Delegates — which, unsurprisingly, are the only ones elected by Puerto Ricans).

Because the past is always present.

This chapter will discuss the takeover of the Puerto Rico government by this Board (what is called a coup d'état in other latitudes).

## The Reason

The bill's Legislative Summary imputes "the situation in Puerto Rico" to three factors:[2]

- fiscal mismanagement
- inconsistent federal policies
- a state-run economy hopelessly inefficient

Since according to the Committee, the political constraints on the economy do not have any effect on the shortfall of government revenues or the contraction of the Puerto Rico economy, the Committee believes that with efficiencies, greater accountability in government operations, optimizing revenues over expenses, and improving the reliability of services, things (I dare not say the economy) will turn around and all will be well.

None so blind as those who will not see.

And I will confess, when I read that bit of the "state-run economy hopelessly inefficient,"[3] I remembered the $37 screw, the $7,622 coffee maker, the $436 hammer, and the $640 toilet seat. Remember those articles bought oh-so-cheaply by the U.S. government-run Pentagon?[4] The agency that, even with its proven inefficient and wasteful management still manages to be the biggest recipient of the U.S.'s taxpayer money?

The Puerto Rico government has never made those kind of purchases.

Let's discuss the supra-government.

## The Schedule and the Access

The Board will establish a schedule for the preparation, submittal, review and certification of the Fiscal Plan and the budgets. There is also a requirement for the submittal of the revenue forecasts. The bill is not clear on this point: it seems the Governor and Legislature will submit these forecasts, but they do not seem to be subject to review independently from the budgets and Fiscal Plan.

As part of the Board's unlimited oversight, it is granted direct access to information systems and all kinds of documents and records as it deems necessary (which includes direct access to automated information systems).

> I get nightmares thinking of the security issues, starting with who will be given access, and to what.

## First, the Fiscal Plan

The bill calls on the Governor to prepare a Fiscal Plan of at least five years, and to submit it to the Board for approval and certification. This Fiscal Plan is the basis for every analysis and authorization that the Board will make (and there are plenty of those).

If the Board finds the Fiscal Plan acceptable, it will issue a certification of compliance. If the Board does not certify the Fiscal Plan, the Governor may revise it by implementing the "corrective" action identified by the Board. If the Fiscal

Plan still does not comply, in the Board's sole discretion, the Board will prepare it and submit it to the Governor and Legislature. In that case, the Fiscal Plan will be deemed approved by the Governor.

> Note this: the Fiscal Plan is "deemed approved" by the Governor. This is a crude attempt to hide that the Fiscal Plan was prepared and imposed by a foreign entity not elected by Puerto Ricans.

The Fiscal Plan:

- Provides for estimates of revenues and expenditures in conformance with modified accrual accounting standards.
- Ensures the funding of essential public services.
- Provides adequate funding for public pension systems.
- Provides for the elimination of budget gaps in financing.
- Provides for a debt burden that is sustainable.
- Improves fiscal governance.
- Enables the achievement of fiscal targets.
- Creates independent forecasts of revenue.

Nothing is required in the Fiscal Plan regarding economic development plans or related policies, which are indispensable for the growth of Puerto Rico's economy and, therefore, its revenue base.

The draft of 24 March required that the Fiscal Plan and Budget include provisions for changes in personnel policies and levels for each department and agency, as well as changes in the structure and organization of the Puerto Rico government.[5] This was eliminated from the draft of 29 March.

## THEN, THE BUDGET

For practical purposes, the Board must have certified the Fiscal Plan for a fiscal year before the Governor can start the process of preparing a Budget. The Governor must submit a Budget to the Board for approval every fiscal year before it is submitted to the Legislature. The Board will determine if the Budget complies with that year's Fiscal Plan.

If it does, the Governor will be authorized to send it to the Legislature. If the Board does not certify the Budget, the Governor may revise it by implementing the "corrective" action identified by the Board. If the Budget still does not comply, the Board will prepare it and submit it to the Governor and Legislature.

The same process applies after the Legislature approves the Budget. If the Board does not consider the Budget compliant with the Fiscal Plan, and the Legislature does not submit one by the first day of the fiscal year, the Board will submit it to the Governor and Legislature and the Budget will be deemed approved by the Governor and Legislature.

> Again note: the Budget is "deemed approved" by the elected government representatives. Another attempt to hide that the Budget was prepared and imposed by a foreign entity not elected by Puerto Ricans.

## REPORTS EVERYWHERE

Every quarter, the Governor must submit to the Board a report that compares actual cash revenues, cash expenditures, and cash flows of the government to the Budget. The Board may require that the information be presented for each "covered territorial instrumentality."

Now, another "threat:" if this quarterly report shows a variance, the Board must report it to the U.S. President and the U.S. Congress, unless Puerto Rico adopts remedial actions (that are acceptable to the Board, of course) and submits monthly reports, instead of quarterly.

The Board must also submit annual reports to the U.S. Congress describing Puerto Rico's progress implementing the bill, and the assistance provided by the Board ("assistance" that I understand to mean a description of the control it exercised over every aspect of the government).

## ... AND CUTS!

If the Governor or the Legislature does not correct a "violation" of actual revenues or expenses against budgeted revenues or expenses, the Board is authorized to make across-the-board reductions in nondebt expenditures to ensure compliance.

> The U.S. Congress is clear on which payments are sacrosanct: notice that cuts are authorized only on nondebt expenditures. What this provision does is alter the flow of funds of the bond indentures and documents under which the debt was issued.

If in an indenture the flow of funds provided for the payment of the bonds after the payment of all other expenses, including operational expenses (which some do), creditors bought that debt knowing they were last in line. Now the U.S. Congress, by altering the protections in the bond documents, is giving preference to the creditors, when the debt documents did not.

## A Takeover

The Board may submit recommendations to the Governor, the Legislature, the U.S. President or the U.S. Congress to "ensure compliance"[6] by Puerto Rico to the Budget and the Fiscal Plan. However, these recommendations may expand to include financial stability, management responsibility, and service delivery efficiency, including recommendations on:

- cost control
- government structure
- additional revenue structures
- alternatives to meet payment of pensions
- privatizations
- changes to Puerto Rico law and Court opinions
- government personnel and lay-offs

Notice a pattern here? The list does not include a single recommendation on anything remotely related to economic development.

> Note also that there are no recommendations on changes to U.S. laws and court opinions that have hobbled Puerto Rico for over a century on economic development, its presence in the global economy, and its participation in international trade.

Now the gloves-off part: the Puerto Rico government has 90 days to implement the recommendations. If it doesn't, it must explain to the U.S. President and the U.S. Congress why it will not implement them.

However, the Board may decide, by the vote of just three members, to implement its own recommendations, but after consulting with the Committee on Natural Resources of the House and the Committee on Energy and Natural Resources of the Senate.

> Because, well, the overlord knows best.

And I ask: are these Committees not busy enough, that they will consult with the Board on whether Puerto Rico should keep its maternity leave act, or what should be the vacation policy for public employees?

Inquiring minds want to know.

[3]

# Elections? For a Government for Puerto Rico? What For?

THE BOARD TAKES OVER the Government of Puerto Rico, for all purposes, in what amounts to the suspension of the Constitution of Puerto Rico.

The first part discussed the process for the approval of fiscal plans and budgets, as well as the reports the Governor must submit to the Board. It also discussed the changes that the Board can make to almost every aspect of life in Puerto Rico, which can be implemented by the vote of three of the Board's members.

## And the Constitution of Puerto Rico Is Suspended

A review of all the powers given to the Board will show that the Constitution of Puerto Rico has been rendered inoperative.

## Laws

The Board must approve every single law approved by the Legislature before it comes into effect.

> Let me repeat that: the Board must approve every single law approved by the Legislature before it comes into effect.

The Board will review each law to see if it is consistent with the Fiscal Plan and the Budget (that the Board has certified) before deciding whether the law will be effective. If the Board, always in its sole discretion, decides that the act is "significantly inconsistent" with the Budget or the Fiscal Plan, the law "shall be null and void."

But the bill provides for this despotic takeover to be a learning experience: "to the extent the Oversight Board considers appropriate, [it shall] provide the Legislature with recommendations for modifications to the Act."[1] Also, if the Board doesn't act in 14 days, the law shall be deemed approved by the Board.

## Contracts and Leases

The same process applies to any contract or lease, no matter the amount: the Board shall examine the transaction and decide whether it is consistent with the Fiscal Plan and the Budget. Only then would the Puerto Rico government be authorized to enter into the agreement. And for this review, the Board has no term to answer.

If it is required, by any existing law or by the Board, the Legislature must approve first any contract or lease before it is submitted to the Board. For example, the bill adds the requirement that the Governor must submit to the Legislature for approval any contract of over $1,000,000. If the Legislature approves the contract, it is submitted to the Board for approval. And then, only if the Board approves it, can the Governor sign the contract or lease.

## Rules and Regulations

The same applies to any rules and regulations proposed by any agency: unless the Board authorizes it, no rules or regulations will enter into effect. Since the bill doesn't specify, and considering that the Legislature must report to the Board and follow its orders, I presume the procedure when dealing with the approval of rules and regulations is this: the agency follows the process established by the Puerto Rico Uniform Administrative Procedures Act, and after it has been complied with, the rule or regulation is submitted to the Board for approval. And the agency has to wait until the Board approves, or disapproves, the rule or regulation, because the Board has no term to answer.

## Governor's Reports

The Governor even has to submit to the Board for review "any report submitted by the Governor for a fiscal year or any quarter," and the Board will review each report and shall submit a report to the U.S. Congress analyzing the completeness and accuracy of the Governor's report.

This, I do not understand. "Any report" means any report submitted by the Governor to any person for any purpose. It would make sense if it referred only to the quarterly reports that the Governor must submit to the Board (there is no requirement for the Governor to submit annual reports to the Board) but, any report? What does that mean?

Also, this section refers to "performance and financial accountability reports" that are not mentioned anywhere else in the bill.

## THE BOARD'S OWN RULES AND REGULATIONS

But that is not all. The Board is authorized to issue the orders, rules, or regulations it considers appropriate to carry out the purposes of the bill, if the Governor or the head of any department or agency could have issued them.

Given this caveat, I believe that the Board would have to follow the Puerto Rico Uniform Administrative Procedures Act, since the Governor or any agency would have had to follow it.

The difference is that the Board must notify the U.S. President and the U.S. Congress if it issues any such orders, rules, or regulations. Another important difference: the orders, rules, or regulations issued by the Board will not be subject to judicial review.

> However, if I read this expansive language of "issue such orders, rules, or regulations it considers

appropriate to carry out the purposes of this Act" along with the authorization to the Board to "ensure [that] the purposes of this Act are met"[2] by cracking down on any attempt from government employees to organize a strike or a lockout, we may very well see an order declaring a state of emergency — issued by the Board.

## The Squeeze Continues

### Borrowing and Reprogramming

Any borrowing by the Puerto Rico government must be approved by the Board. I wonder if that includes capital leases of equipment and machinery, since the bill doesn't provide for any exception.

If the Governor wants to reprogram any amount provided in a Budget, it must receive the approval of the Board before submitting it to the Legislature. Note that this is not a new expense; it is transferring funds from one purpose to another. There is no effect in the total budget, and no increase in expenses.

But since even this minimizes the severe control of the Board over public policy in Puerto Rico, it will not do. So, even the reprogramming of funds within a Budget is subject to "an analysis" by the Board.

Puerto Rico's Constitution is indeed suspended.

## Puerto Rico Judiciary

And now for the missing party: The Judiciary. The bill doesn't mention Puerto Rico's Judiciary at all. Anything related to the bill will be argued before the District Court of the District of Columbia and appealed to the Circuit Court of the District of Columbia. The subpoenas and any restructuring will be litigated before the federal court in Puerto Rico.

Our Judiciary? It is nowhere to be found, except to clarify that the Board's power to issue subpoenas does not extend to "judicial officers or employees of the Puerto Rico courts."

> I sure hope the term "judicial officers" includes the judges.
>
> The Constitution of Puerto Rico goes poof.

## Extra Powers

The Board must approve any discretionary tax waivers granted by the Puerto Rico government. I understand this to mean that tax incentives laws are now under the direct supervision of the Board, since "discretionary tax waivers" would include tax incentive contracts.

The Board is explicitly granted the authorization to take cooperative efforts with Puerto Rico, including recommending changes to Federal laws or actions of the Federal Government, that would help Puerto Rico in complying with the Fiscal Plan and Budgets.

Who knows whether this includes changes in the Federal laws that impose constraints on Puerto Rico's economic development.

## And When Does This Start?

Any of these six events would start an "oversight period":[3]

1. The failure by the central government, any agency or any public corporation to provide sufficient revenue to a debt service reserve fund.
2. A default on any form of borrowing.
3. The failure of the Puerto Rico government to meet its payroll.
4. The existence of a cash deficit at the end of any quarter.
5. The failure to make required payments related to pensions and benefits.
6. The failure to make payments to any entity established under an interstate compact.

The "oversight period" ends when the Board certifies that both:

1. Puerto Rico has adequate access to short-term and long-term credit at reasonable interest rates.
2. The expenditures made during each year did not exceed the revenues for five consecutive fiscal years.

However, the events that signal the start of an oversight period are not immediately important, since the bill deems that an oversight period exists right now.

## Eternally Watchful

But the Board's work is never done. Even if there is no oversight period, the Governor must keep submitting the government Budget to the Board, forever, so the Board can prepare a report to the U.S. President and the U.S. Congress.

The Board shall also keep monitoring the "financial status" of Puerto Rico (whatever that means, and whatever that implies) so that, if the Board believes there is a risk that an oversight period may start, it can submit a report to the U.S. President and the U.S. Congress.[4]

The bill doesn't clarify what the phrase "a risk exists that an oversight period may be initiated" means. Next fiscal year? Within five years? Possible? Probable?

> Since the Board's oversight is perpetual, I guess they will consider a sliver of risk as enough to recommend the start of an oversight period.

## Distrust

Now, my favorite section of the bill. If the Fiscal Plan and Budget are prepared by consensus among the Board, the Governor, and the Legislature, the Board must certify that the Budget and the Fiscal Plan reflect a consensus...

...and must send copy to the U.S. President and the U.S. Congress.

If the Board certifies the Fiscal Plan or the Budget under the process of review, reject, revise, approve, and certify, the Board is not required to send a copy to either the U.S. President or the U.S. Congress.

But if the Fiscal Plan and Budget are prepared by consensus? Then it must send a copy to the U.S. President and the U.S. Congress.

> So, the U.S. President and the U.S. Congress can make sure the Board is as controlling as it can be?

## Oh, It Died

Humpty Dumpty sat on a wall,
Humpty Dumpty had a great fall;
all the king's horses and all the king's men
couldn't put Humpty together again.
—MOTHER GOOSE

The Commonwealth of Puerto Rico, as a constitutional body, lies pulverized.

We wish it peace in the afterlife.

## Elections and Self-Governance

There is no need to celebrate elections in Puerto Rico this November. An election to install a government that is, for all intents and purposes, an employee of this Board?

This bill does away with the Constitution of Puerto Rico. The setting of public policy, the control over budget, infrastructure expenditure, restructuring of its debt, the policies and legal framework that reflect Puerto Ricans' social priorities, are all hijacked by a Board appointed by the U.S. President, and for whom we Puerto Ricans do not vote.

The Committee tries to make us believe that the Board will exercise its control in "the most efficient and equitable manner that is respectful of the rule of law, self-governance..."[5]

That is impossible.

A Board that controls every single aspect of the Puerto Rico government and Puerto Ricans' life does not respect self-governance. When just three people named by the U.S. President with no input whatsoever from Puerto Ricans can make changes to our government, our laws, our policies, our resources, and our assets, there is no self-governance.

> That has many names; self-governance is not one of them.

So, elections? In Puerto Rico? In November? What for? To elect an inefficacious government that will be nothing more than a subordinate of this Board?

> I look forward to reading the reports to be filed by the U.S. before the Decolonization Committee of the United Nations, again, considering this bill annihilates the Constitution of Puerto Rico.

## FORAKER 21

It is clear, though, that the Congressional dilly-dallying is over. November is close, Puerto Ricans do not vote but creditors do, and politicians believe, above all, in self-preservation.

Even so, it flabbergasts me that the U.S. Congress would draft something like this.

Reading the bill I thought of what Professor T. Alexander Aleinikoff called "the imperialistic fires burning in the nation."[6] See the pains Congress takes to make clear that "Nothing in this Act may be construed ... to limit the authority of Congress to exercise ultimate legislative authority over Puerto Rico."[7]

> Yep, the U.S. Supreme Court has everyone very, very nervous. Goodness, what if it held that the approval of the Constitution of Puerto Rico placed Puerto Rico outside of the territorial clause? Oh no, no, no! See Chapter 9 for a brief discussion.

Since with this bill the U.S. Congress has shown how willing it is to annul the Constitution of Puerto Rico (always under the let-us-use-it-now-maybe-soon-will-die territorial clause), a more appropriate name for this bill would be "The Foraker Act for the New Century," especially since the Foraker Act of 1900 is the spiritual parent of this PROMESA.[8] Its short name could be "Foraker 21."

The coveted control over budgets, expenses, government structure, legislation, contracts, assets, and life in general is still possible — just like it was 116 years ago.

Another advantage of calling it Foraker 21? There is no need for acronyms.

Back to the future indeed.

## Ever Present

How much of this aggressive pursuit of the crude implementation of the plenary power of the territorial clause is because of the escalation of hostilities with the ones "over there far away," is for the people in the five-sided building to know ... and for us in Puerto Rico to never ignore.[9]

# [4]

# An Ordered, Fair Debt Restructuring

BY NOW IT IS accepted that payments on Puerto Rico debt cannot be made, and that a rational proposal to approve a debt restructuring process should be enacted. The PROMESA attempts to do that.

It also tries to deliver a preemptive strike, in case the U.S. Supreme Court decided to grant some restructuring powers to Puerto Rico.

Since everyone has apparently discarded following the provisions of the bond documents, then, as a secondary alternative, it makes sense to create a restructuring process similar to what is familiar to most U.S. bondholders.

## Puerto Rico Debt

Puerto Rico debt is quite interesting. Puerto Rico government debt has been issued under Puerto Rico laws and subject to Puerto Rico courts. Some documents provide for the exclusive jurisdiction of Puerto Rico courts. The Puerto Rico Supreme Court has never interpreted any of the bond documents or its provisions.

Matters get complicated since U.S. bondholders, although having bought this debt that is subject to Puerto Rico law and courts, do not want to litigate in Puerto Rico courts, much less would like to apply Puerto Rico law to their bond holdings.

Creditors have used their quite-effective lobbyists to convince Congress that a restructuring process subject to Federal laws and litigated in Federal courts, and directed by a group named by the U.S. government, is in their best interest. (Although, by declarations some of them have made in the press,[1] the bill does not seem to be as protective of their best interests as they had hoped.)

This chapter will discuss:

- the bill's provisions on voluntary agreements for debt adjustment
- the stay on claims against Puerto Rico debtors
- the proposed process for the filing of a petition for an adjustment of debt under Title III of the PROMESA.

## The Board's Members

The bill requires that Members of the Financial Oversight and Management Board do not have any other conflict of interest, including owning any debt securities of Puerto Rico.

That makes a lot of sense, particularly since the bill makes the Board the agent and trustee of Puerto Rico for any restructuring process that may start under the process created by the bill's Title III.

However, I find it intriguing that this requirement is marked as temporary language. True, this is a draft. But, since this requirement is fundamental, I find it remarkable that it is presented as just a possibility.

My skepticism is alive and well.

## THE STAY, OR LET (IT) BREATHE

The bill provides for the stay of all claims against Puerto Rico debtors the moment the Board is established. The stay applies to all entities. This means that no person, estate, trust, governmental unit, or U.S. trustee can:

- Start an action or proceeding against the Puerto Rico government that could have been started before the PROMESA was enacted.
- Continue one that was started before the PROMESA was enacted.
- Start an action or proceeding to recover a claim against the Puerto Rico government that was created before the PROMESA was enacted.
- Enforce a judgment obtained before the PROMESA was enacted.
- Obtain possession or exercise control over property of the Puerto Rico government.

- Create, perfect, or enforce any lien against property of the Puerto Rico government.
- Collect, assess, or recover a bond claim against the Puerto Rico government.
- Setoff of any debt owing to the Puerto Rico government.

However, the stay does not apply to processes of a judicial or administrative nature, or any other action or proceeding against the Puerto Rico government, that started on or before 18 December 2015. (That day the Puerto Rico Electric Power Authority reached a tentative agreement to restructure its debt with a group of insurance companies and creditors, and the bill lets it run its course.)

The stay lasts for 18 months, or until a petition is filed under Title III, whichever comes first.

The only court with jurisdiction is the Federal District Court of Puerto Rico.

The bill also prohibits that contracts with the Puerto Rico government be terminated because of a provision of insolvency. That means that if a contract stated it would be terminated if the Puerto Rico government was found insolvent, that provision will not be effective, and the party has to keep complying with the contract, as long as the government complies with all the other terms.

## They Will Agree

The bill requires that the Board certify any voluntary agreement that the Puerto Rico government has "consummated" with debt holders to restructure the debt. Without that certification, the agreement will not be effective. The Board must certify both that the agreement:

1. Provides for a sustainable level of debt.
2. Conforms with the Fiscal Plan.

The 24 March draft used "successfully reached"[2] instead of "consummated." I wonder if the change in terms means that now the restructuring agreement must be signed and executed before the Board examines the terms.

> I think it is probable, since for other reviews and analyses the Board makes, the bill requires the transaction be submitted to the Board in final form.
>
> I do not think the purpose of the change is to wait until the obligations of the parties under the agreement have been completed, because that would take years. Using "consummated" makes sense if what is meant is that the final agreement has been reached and the parties are clear as to each other's responsibilities.

## The Certification

The Board must certify, before filing any petition and plan of adjustment on behalf of a debtor of the Puerto Rico government, that both the petition and the plan are consistent with the Fiscal Plan.

The Board is authorized to issue a "restructuring certification" to a government entity under certain circumstances:

- The Puerto Rico government has made reasonable effort to reach a voluntary agreement that conforms with the Fiscal Plan.
- The entity has adopted procedures to deliver timely audited financial statements and draft financial statements.
- The entity has adopted procedures to deliver timely other information sufficient for any interested party to perform due diligence on the entity's financial condition.

Under exigent circumstances the Board may file a petition for restructuring, even if these conditions are not met.

This language needs work. The Puerto Rico debtor has to comply with these requirements before the Board would consider filing a restructuring petition on the debtor's behalf. The bill should state that the Board has to either "conclude the requirements were met," or the certification is part of the petition that the Board would file on behalf of the debtor.

It makes no sense to issue a "restructuring certification" to a debtor that cannot file a restructuring petition, since the filing of the petition is in the Board's discretion, and the restructuring process is under the Board's control.

## THE PROCESS YOU WATCH

Title III of the bill creates a process for the adjustment of debt of a territory, which includes Puerto Rico in the definition. Section 301 of the PROMESA lists the sections of the Bankruptcy Code that apply to the proceedings created for the territories.

The petition is filed with the Federal District Court in Puerto Rico, but — a big but — if the Board decides that this court will not adequately provide for proper case management, then it may transfer the case to the Federal court of the District of Columbia, because that is where the Board's other office is located.

How do you like that?

Whichever court, Puerto Rico or District of Columbia, may not interfere with:

- any of the political or governmental powers of the debtor
- any of the property or revenues of the debtor
- the use or enjoyment by the debtor of any income-producing property

The bill clarifies that an affiliate of a debtor includes Puerto Rico's central government and all instrumentalities of Puerto Rico. Therefore, all debtors of the Puerto Rico government are affiliates of each other.

That means that the Board may file petitions and plans of adjustments jointly for all of them: in theory, all of the debt issued by the Puerto Rico government could be tackled in the same plan of adjustment.

As a preemptive strike against any opinion of the U.S. Supreme Court favorable to Puerto Rico on the validity of Puerto Rico's Recovery Act,[3] the bill states that no law approved by a territory may bind any creditor that does not consent to the composition of debt. (Composition of debt is when debtors and creditors agree to new terms of repayment, or to repayment in full for less than the full amount owed.)

Only the Board may file a petition and a plan of adjustment under this Title III and may take any action necessary on behalf of Puerto Rico to prosecute the case, including filing a petition, and submitting or modifying a plan of adjustment. The bill doesn't mention preparing either the petition or the plan, and neither does it state anything about what Puerto Rico's participation will be in this process.

> But since the bill makes clear that Title III cannot be understood to limit the powers of the Board granted by the U.S. Congress in any manner whatsoever, I do not think Puerto Rico will be allowed to be an active participant.

### Other Territories

A territory may not be a debtor under this Title III unless it is subject to a Board.

Therefore, although the definition of territories includes Guam, the Northern Mariana Islands, American Samoa, and the U.S. Virgin Islands, none of them may use this process unless and until the U.S. Congress enacts an Act subjecting them to a Board. In practical terms, this bill should have no effect whatsoever on the market for their bonds.

## THE ATTEMPT

In an attempt to respect Puerto Rico's Judiciary, the bill requires that the Federal court abstain from determining an issue requiring an opinion on:

- interests in property under the laws of Puerto Rico
- interpretation or application of the Constitution of Puerto Rico

Only if the Puerto Rico Supreme Court has issued a controlling decision on the issue at hand, may the Federal court decide. But if the Supreme Court has not, the Federal court must certify the issue to the Puerto Rico Supreme Court (it has to inform the Supreme Court of the issue so the Supreme Court can issue the opinion on Puerto Rico law that will be binding upon all courts — except, of course, the U.S. Supreme Court).

Since about 95% of debt issued by Puerto Rico is subject to and must be interpreted under Puerto Rico law, this is quite reasonable. Especially because the Puerto Rico Supreme Court has not issued "controlling decisions" on bond documents, nor on most of the laws, rules, and regulations applicable to bond issues.

> This mandatory abstention is indispensable so Puerto Rico debtors benefit from the protections that they very prudently included in all of their bond documents.

## All's Well

The applicable Federal court (Puerto Rico or District of Columbia) must confirm a plan of adjustment filed by the Board if it meets with all of these conditions:

- The plan complies with the process established by the PROMESA in its section 301.
- The plan complies with the provisions of Title III.
- All amounts paid or owed by the debtor for services or expenses in the case or related to the plan of adjustment have been disclosed and are reasonable.
- The debtor is not prohibited by law from taking any action necessary to carry out the plan.
- Administrative expenses, fees, and costs have been paid in full, in cash.
- Any regulatory or electoral approval necessary in order to carry out any provision of the plan has been obtained.
- The plan is in the best interests of creditors and is feasible.
- The plan is consistent with the Fiscal Plan certified by the Board.

## Is All This in Vain?

The bill has a dangerous section that seems to put in jeopardy all processes taken under Title III:

> Nothing in this Act may be construed (1) to relieve any obligations existing as of the date of the enactment of this Act of the Government of Puerto Rico to repay any individual or entity from whom Puerto Rico has borrowed funds, whether through the issuance of bonds or otherwise;[4]

"Nothing in this Act" includes Title III. What is the purpose of this paragraph? If it wants to exclude just the processes, actions, and proceedings started on or before 18 December 2015 it must say so.

## Sovereignty and Finance

The intersection of finance and sovereignty (or even self-governance, to use the congressional term) is nowhere clearer than in Puerto Rico.

This Title III could be an attempt at a solution. I find it difficult to call it a fair attempt because Puerto Rico does not appear to be a party in the pre-filing process, and it is subject to the Board's decisions since the Board is its agent and trustee.

Title III does a pretty good job in preserving the applicability of Puerto Rico's law, even if the attempt is not very elegant because of the political constraints on status and the U.S.'s interest in preserving it.

In general, I consider Title III an acceptable attempt.

Nevertheless, I like history enough to know that I should not stop looking for a trap in there somewhere.

[5]

# The Privatization Czar

THE "PUERTO RICO REVITALIZATION ACT" provides for the appointment of a Revitalization Coordinator who will be in charge of negotiating the privatization of all salable assets that belong to Puerto Rico. The privatization would be under a special process applicable to declared emergencies. It is Title V of the PROMESA.

The Revitalization Coordinator has sole discretion to determine whether an offer received for the privatization of an asset should proceed.

The Puerto Rico government? It decides nothing.

We have a Board appointed by the U.S. President selecting a privatization czar that has the final word on the sale of assets belonging to Puerto Rico.

My discussion of the "Puerto Rico Revitalization Act" includes:

- The appointment and powers of the Revitalization Coordinator
- Puerto Rico Act 76-2000
- The privatization process under Title V of the PROMESA
- Greece's privatization program

## THE SET-UP

The Committee's Legislative Summary for the PROMESA shares the finding that "over the past few months the Committee's oversight efforts have revealed a desire to privately invest in Puerto Rico."[1]

> It does not take months of a Congressional Committee's oversight to know that there is a desire to privately invest in Puerto Rico. That has never been in doubt.
>
> The question is under what terms that "desire" is interested.

A little recent history: in April 2015 and July 2015 several bondholders of the Puerto Rico Electric and Power Authority offered iterations of a private investment plan. Not much of the plan was made public, but one feature was that it would not be subject to competitive bidding processes. PREPA rejected them because, among other reasons, they were unacceptable to other creditors, including debt insurers.

For the proposed plans, the bondholders had selected providers of services, equipment, infrastructure, and financing, and presented the new privatization of energy generation as an accomplished fact.

Now Title V focuses on the privatization of PREPA, and mostly on the generation aspect of the electric service.

> What a coincidence! That was the subject of the privatization offer made by the PREPA bondholders, who have also been very active in their lobbying efforts in Congress.

As I will discuss, the PROMESA adopts the PREPA creditors' method of presenting proposals.

## The Gifts (That Will Keep on Giving?)

The PROMESA authorizes the Board to:

> accept, use, and dispose of gifts, bequests, or devises of services or property, both real and personal, for the purpose of aiding or facilitating the work of the Oversight Board.[2]

The Board will deposit these "gifts, bequests, or devises of money and proceeds from sales of other property received as gifts, bequests, or devises"[3] in an account in the Board's name and will disburse them under the Board's rules and regulations.

Notice that? The Board who selects the Revitalization Coordinator and approves all privatization transactions is authorized to receive gifts of services and property if, in its sole discretion, they aid or facilitate the work of the Board. And these moneys will then be used by the Board as it, in its sole discretion, sees fit.

And Congress sees no problem with this? Goodness!

## THE CZAR

This Revitalization Act eliminates any bidding process in the sale of assets belonging to Puerto Rico, and puts all sales solely in the hands of persons appointed by the U.S. President.

The Revitalization Coordinator is "appointed" by the Governor from the candidates selected by the Board.

These are the qualifications required from this privatization czar:

- substantial knowledge and expertise in the planning, pre-development, financing and development of infrastructure projects, provided that stronger consideration shall be given to candidates who have experience with energy infrastructure projects;
- does not currently provide, or in the preceding three calendar years provided, goods or services to the government of Puerto Rico (and is not the spouse, parent, child, or sibling of an individual who provides or has provided goods and services to the

government of Puerto Rico in the preceding three calendar years); and

- is not an officer, employee of, or former officer or employee of the government of Puerto Rico in the preceding three calendar years.

Everyone familiar with political parties and politicians in Puerto Rico will recognize that this is an attempt to disqualify every single person that has provided services to this administration, affiliated with the U.S. Democratic Party, and to make eligible persons who worked under the prior administration, whose Governor has always been affiliated to the U.S. Republican Party.

It is impossible to be any more obvious — unless the bill actually named names.

## The Buffet. I Mean, the Critical Projects

Any "project sponsor" (the bill does not define the term, so I take it to mean any person) may submit a proposed project to the Coordinator and the relevant agency from the Puerto Rico government.

The proposal is submitted so that the project be considered a "critical project." This way, it could benefit from the expedited permitting and the provisions of privatization of the PROMESA.

Title V defines a "critical project" as one that:

- is defined as a "critical project" by Title V; and
- is "intimately related to addressing an emergency, as defined by Section 1 of Act 76."

"Act 76" refers to the Puerto Rico Act 76-2000.[4]

This second requirement is confusing, since this Puerto Rico Revitalization Act includes its own definition of "emergency." Or does it refer to the Act 76-2000's definition of what is "intimately related"?

The proposal must:

- Describe the impact the proposed project will have on an emergency (whether as defined by Act 76-2000 or this Puerto Rico Revitalization Act is not clear).
- Notify the availability of immediate private capital.
- Detail economic benefits, including number of jobs.
- If it is an existing or ongoing project, describe its status.
- Meet any additional criteria the Coordinator and the Board deem appropriate.

I do not understand the reference to an "ongoing project." If it is ongoing it must have complied with all permits and legal requirements already. Otherwise, it could not have started.

What is the purpose of the language? Who does it want to benefit?

## ENERGY IS ALL WE NEED

If a proposed project is an "energy project" it needs to submit six additional requirements, which are explanations on how the project:

- Reduces reliance on oil for electric generation.
- Improves energy infrastructure and efficiency.
- Expedites diversification and conversion to natural gas and renewable.
- Develops the utilization of energy sources found on Puerto Rico.
- Helps the transition to privatized generation.
- Meets additional criteria the Coordinator and the Board deem appropriate.

"Energy projects" has an incredibly broad definition: "those that address the generation, distribution, or transmission of energy, natural gas, and similar fuels."[5]

Let me make just one comment:

Puerto Rico has been transitioning to natural gas as one of its energy sources. Do you know what is a big hurdle? The Jones Act of 1920.[6] The U.S. Merchant Marine does not have vessels that can transport natural gas.

> So Puerto Rico cannot buy natural gas from the U.S., even if those producers had the cheapest prices: no ships can legally transport it to Puerto Rico.

## What Is an Emergency?

To qualify as a "critical project" that will benefit from the fast-track privatization process, a project proposal must be "intimately related to addressing an emergency, as defined by section 1 of [Puerto Rico] Act 76-2000."[7]

Act 76-2000 was enacted to exempt government agencies involved in the permitting process from complying with the terms and procedures established in several laws, for projects that arise as a result of a state of emergency declared by the Governor.

Act 76-2000 defines an emergency as:

> any serious abnormality such as a hurricane, tidal wave, earthquake, volcanic eruption, drought, fire, explosion, or any other kind of catastrophe, or any serious disruption of the public law and order, or an attack by enemy forces through sabotage or through the use of bombs, artillery or explosives of any nature, or by atomic, radiological, chemical, or bacteriological means, or by any other means that the enemy may use in any part of the territory of the Commonwealth of Puerto Rico, that merits the mobilization and extraordinary use of human and economic resources to remedy, avoid, prevent or diminish the severity or magnitude of the damages caused or that could be caused. Likewise, the term 'emergency' covers any event or grave problems of deterioration in the physical infrastructure for the rendering of essential services to the people, or that endangers the life, public health, or safety of the population or of a sensitive ecosystem.[8]

Act 76-2000 requires that the Executive Order issued by the Governor set the criteria and parameters that will apply to the emergency. It "shall establish the geographic area, the intensity and extent of the damages, and the public works or government function that must be urgently reinforced or protected."[9]

Based on the Executive Order, the agencies are authorized to establish alternate procedures and terms to expedite permits, endorsements, consultations, and certifications related to the solution of the emergency declared by the Governor.

This is applicable for the duration of the emergency, and applies to "works that are intimately related to the problem, or that respond to an immediate solution to the situation created by the emergency."[10]

## The Perversion

Compare the definition of "emergency" in Act 76-2000 to the definition in this Puerto Rico Revitalization Act:

> means any event or grave problem of deterioration in the physical infrastructure for the rendering of essential services to the people, or that endangers the life, public health, or safety of the population or of a sensitive ecosystem. This shall include problems in the physical infrastructure for energy, water, sewer, solid waste, highways or roads, ports, telecommunications and other similar infrastructure.[11]

This bill uses as the basis for its "expedited permitting process" the Puerto Rico Act 76-2000. It even quotes the last sentence of the Act's definition of an emergency to justify the increase in the number of projects that would qualify for this expedited process.

Act 76-2000 was enacted to enable the Governor to swiftly react to emergencies created by hurricanes, floods, droughts, earthquakes, tidal waves, and the like. The law's definition of emergency and infrastructure deterioration is in this context. Think, for example, of bridges that collapse during a hurricane.

The Governor must establish a geographic area for the emergency, the extent of the damages, and identify the public works that must be repaired.

The PROMESA takes that language, strips it of context, and includes it in this Title V as if the infrastructure deterioration was, by itself, enough to justify an emergency. Then Congress has the audacity of using the Act 76-2000 as a cover to violate the permitting and public bidding laws in Puerto Rico.

> And all this, to sell property that belongs to Puerto Rico!

And to make sure every "project sponsor" knows what is available, the PROMESA's definition of emergency includes infrastructure for energy, water, sewer, solid waste, highways or roads, ports, telecommunications and other similar infrastructure.

What a perversion.

## Your Laws Don't Give Me What I Want

There are laws in Puerto Rico to carry out projects of the kind contemplated in this title. It is only in an emergency that these processes change, because the situation is dire and extraordinary, and the life, public health, or safety of Puerto Ricans is at immediate risk.

Puerto Rico also has a Public-Private Partnership Act[12] under which these kinds of transactions are meant to be evaluated and consummated. But that law requires public participation, and hearings, and viability studies, and public bidding. It is not a privatization act, because it does not authorize the transfer of a government asset's ownership to a private party.

But this PROMESA provides for the sale of Puerto Rico assets, and on fast-track.

## The Intriguing Transfer

The PROMESA provides for the transfer to Puerto Rico of the land in Vieques (an island municipality) that the Department of Defense had transferred to the U.S. Department of the Interior in 2001.

This transfer was the result of the Puerto Rico protests and efforts to stop the 60-year bombing of Vieques by the U.S. Navy. Congress approved an act transferring part of the land in Vieques that had been under the U.S. Navy jurisdiction to the Department of the Interior.

It also ordered the Department of Defense to clean the land that had been used for bombing of ordnance, hazardous substances, contaminants and pollutants, which include napalm and depleted uranium. That work is ongoing.

Some of the land was transferred by the U.S. Navy to the Puerto Rico government, but it is managed by the U.S. Secretary of the Interior pursuant to a cooperative agreement among Puerto Rico, the Puerto Rico Conservation Trust, and the U.S. Secretary of the Interior.

Intriguingly, the PROMESA authorizes the transfer to Puerto Rico of the land that the Navy had transferred to the Department of the Interior, so that Puerto Rico may use it or further transfer it.

The agreement by the Department of Defense to clean up the land will continue to apply after the transfer. However, and most importantly, it declares that the cooperative agreement with the Department of the Interior will not apply to this newly transferred land.

Let's see:

- The PROMESA transfers to Puerto Rico land that plenty of developers have been "desiring."
- Congress generously gifts Puerto Rico with this property, and authorizes Puerto Rico to transfer it to someone else.
- It also excludes it from the management by the Secretary of the Interior, who is the person that manages the Vieques land that was transferred to the Puerto Rico government.

> Remember how this privatization process works. Almost every Puerto Rico asset is up for grabs, since everything related to energy, water, sewer, solid waste, highways or roads, ports, telecommunications and other similar infrastructure may be subject to a privatization proposal.

So, Congress adds to the buffet and provides that this new land will not be subject to anyone else's management.

> It would make its privatization a nightmare.

## Move, Move, Move

The Puerto Rico government agency must notify the Coordinator the "expedited permitting process" it has approved, which is the process required by Act 76-2000 when the Governor has declared an emergency.

The Coordinator, in consultation with the agency, will decide whether a proposed project complies with the criteria required, and will issue a recommendation to the Board. The recommendation is on whether the project will be considered a "critical project."

If a project is considered "critical," it will have a right to benefit from the "expedited permitting process."

In another one of the strange things in this bill, the recommendation to the Board must include a recommendation by the Governor. However, the bill never sets any procedure for the Coordinator to send neither the proposal information nor its own evaluation of the proposal to the Governor.

Or is it that the consultation the Coordinator carries out with the agencies is concurrent to the recommendation the agency makes to the Governor? I do not understand this.

The Board will make the final decision on whether the project will be a "critical project." The Governor just gives a recommendation.

This Title V requires that the Puerto Rico government agencies operate as if the Governor has issued an Executive Order declaring an emergency under Act 76-2000. The problem is that there is no document:

- establishing the geographic area subject to the emergency
- establishing the intensity and extent of the damages
- identifying the public works or government function that must be urgently reinforced or protected

What guide do the agencies have to design their "expedited permitting process"?

## Governor, Get Out of Our Way

To leave no question about who is in charge of setting and distributing the buffet, the Czar has to approve any action the Governor takes under Section 11 of Act 76-2000.

This section authorizes the Governor to approve, amend and revoke regulations and Executive Orders, and cancel the contracts that it deems necessary during the emergency.

If the Coordinator does not approve an action taken by the Governor, the decision must be reviewed by the Board. If the Board agrees with the Coordinator, the action taken by the Governor is null and void.

> So, there it is, again.
>
> A Coordinator and a Board appointed by the U.S. President order about the elected Governor of Puerto Rico.

## THE CONTROL NEVER ENDS

The hobbled Legislature is required to submit to the Coordinator and the Board any legislation that may affect any "expedited permitting process." And again, if the Board considers it hinders the expedited process, the proposed legislation is dead on arrival.

Now, to the agencies. They cannot include any term or condition that is not required, if the Revitalization Coordinator determines it would prevent or impair the expeditious construction, operation, or expansion of a "critical project."

The additional requirements that the Puerto Rico laws left to the expertise of the agency cannot be included in any "critical project" if the Coordinator, in its sole discretion, decides that it would hurt the expeditiousness of any project he deems critical.

> Apparently, Congress doesn't think there is place for expertise in this fire-sale of Puerto Rico assets.

## They Do Not Count

As with the other titles of the bill, the Federal court in Puerto Rico is the only court with jurisdiction to determine the validity of actions taken under this Title V.

And, as is usual in this PROMESA, another reminder: "The provisions of this title shall prevail over any general or special provision of Puerto Rican law or regulation that is inconsistent therewith."[13]

> Back to the future with a U.S. President-appointed government, with unlimited powers and discretion, like the Foraker Act of 1900.

## The Cynicism

Please be clear: every decision by the Board is taken by a majority vote; that is, the vote of three members. Three persons appointed by the U.S. President with no participation from Puerto Ricans make every decision under the PROMESA, over the representatives elected by Puerto Ricans.

We do not vote for the U.S. President. We do not have representatives in Congress.

And, to top it all off, the PROMESA is cynic enough to declare the:

> national interest of enhancing Puerto Rico's infrastructure for electricity, water and sewer services, roads and bridges, ports, and solid waste management to achieve compliance with local and federal environmental laws, regulations and policies while ensuring the continuity of adequate services to the people of Puerto Rico and the Commonwealth's sustainable economic development.[14]

From that language, this is what I understand: that it is in the U.S. national interest:

- to squeeze Puerto Ricans with unlimited austerity
- while granting U.S. interested parties a fire-sale process of Puerto Rico assets
- conducted by a czar appointed by non-elected persons

Foraker 21.

## EVER PRESENT

This Title V of the PROMESA may be a reflection of the belief of its authors that the private sector does it better. It could be a help to the bondholders whose proposal to PREPA was rejected and now will be given someone more sympathetic to negotiate with.

> But I also wonder if this rush to privatize the infrastructure in Puerto Rico for energy, water, highways, roads, ports, and telecommunications may be because it is easier for the U.S. Department of Defense to interact and reach agreements with private parties than with the Puerto Rico government.

## Privatization Spree, Greek Style

Under its agreement for assistance with the International Monetary Fund and other creditors, Greece presented a proposal to privatize a lot of its major and vital national assets and infrastructure. The proposal was made under the pressure of its creditors, and included assets that the creditors had requested be privatized.

Greece created a privatization authority, the Hellenic Republic Asset Development Fund, that oversees the Hellenic Republic Privatization Program. Its members are selected by the Greek Parliament, although there are two observers from the Eurozone Member States. The Asset Development Fund uses the moneys it receives from the privatizations to reduce Greece's debt.

As you can see, the Greek government is in charge of its privatization program. Even if its creditors are breathing down its neck.

## Need Help?

It has been made clear that what the U.S. private investors need to do when they cannot convince the Puerto Rico government to accede to their terms for privatization is go to Congress. So they can be given by Congressional law what they cannot get by negotiation. Sweet, sweet deal.

Back to the future.

# [PART 2]

## Version of 12 April 2016

[6]

# Less "Colonialist"? I Don't Think So

"'AMERICAN CITIZENS LIVING IN Puerto Rico' we worry about you! So much so, that we want to squeeze you to death!"

Wink, wink.

On 12 April 2016 the newest, less "colonialist" (Congress's word), version of the PROMESA, H.R. 4900,[1] was made public: the bill I refer to as Foraker 21 for its regression to the early 20th century days of a U.S. President-appointed government for Puerto Rico.

There is a little more common sense in version 2 (Foraker 21, version 2) than there was in version 1 (F1).

On the other hand, since the Title V on restructuring on debt made pretty good sense, it was gutted.

No surprises there.

This chapter will discuss the changes from the F1 to the F2.

## The Other

I'll start with what I am grateful for in this version: honesty on the part of the Republican Congressmen who have made it very clear that there are Americans, and then there are "American citizens living in Puerto Rico."[2] It is honest of them to say that they do not consider us to be the same.

The summary[3] of this newest version of the bill and the press[4] releases[5] make very clear that risks to Americans who bought Puerto Rico debt will be mitigated to the highest extent possible, because risks for Americans stemming from Puerto Rico debt will not be tolerated.

Because, you see, there are issuers — and there are issuers. American issuers are protected by the Bankruptcy Code, and their American purchasers are subject to the losses imposed upon them by the American Bankruptcy Code.

> No Member of Congress would ever dare say that the loss suffered by the American buyer of an American issuer through an American bankruptcy proceeding was a bailout by the American taxpayer to the American issuer.

But Puerto Rico issuers are not American issuers. And these Congressmen are using clear words to say it, so that no one with a smidgen of reason will miss the message.

"American citizens living in Puerto Rico" are low in the pecking order — if we are even on the list.

Whoever was expecting something else, better finally wake up. Clear language helps to set expectations for the future.

Now, to the language that cements the difference: the colonialist angle.

To my surprise, Congress has dared use the concept of colonialism. The one-page summary[5] states that the "Board language" was "modified" "to address concerns that it was too colonialist."[6]

I'm still in shock. Never thought I'd see the day.

## THE BACKGROUND

Congress still refuses to clearly state that the constraints imposed by the political status have a negative impact on Puerto Rico's economic growth prospects. However, in the bill's internet page,[7] the Committee is willing to finally recognize that one of the causes of this crisis is the "burdensome federal regulatory policy."[8] You will see that the two places of honor in the list belong to the Puerto Rico Electric Power Authority, but that priority is more a reflection of some creditors' interests in PREPA than reality.

Sure, that phrase about "burdensome federal regulatory policy" could refer exclusively to the minimum wage and not to anything else, but even if Congress refuses to admit it more explicitly, the laws it approves are extremely burdensome for Puerto Rico.[9]

Let's get to the changes.

> I'm analyzing the version of F2 marked 1:43 p.m., 12 April 2016.

## The Board

These are the changes from the F1 to the F2:

- The number of members of the Board increased. Instead of five, they are now seven, so that the Minority Leaders of each chamber can propose a list from which the U.S. President must elect one member.
- However, to counteract this change, the votes needed vary by action, instead of a simple majority as before.
- The Secretary of the Treasury was removed as member of the Board.
- The qualifications to be a member of the Board have not changed, except that it now includes "municipal bond markets" as one of the areas of expertise that can be considered in a candidate.
- A new paragraph authorizes executive sessions of the Board, closed to the public.
- The second office of the Board doesn't have to be in District of Columbia anymore. It may be anywhere the Board sees fit. Actually, it may have additional offices, plural.

Now, let us all sing, New York, New York!

Wait until we discuss the changes to the courts in charge of the restructuring process, and you will see why.

- Eliminates all the references to the rights reserved to federal employees that would transfer to work for the Board, as well as the incorporation of the employees recruited by the Board in some federal employee programs.
- The Board may still accept gifts, but the F2 now requires that the gifts and the identities of the donors be made public within 30 days.

I shudder thinking about the many transactions that can close in 30 days.

- Adds a section requiring the Board and its staff to comply with the federal conflicts of interest requirements, as well as the financial disclosure requirements.[10]

Although this F2 refers to "the Federal conflict of interest requirements described in section 2018 of Title 18, United States Code," the correct reference should be to section 208. Section 2018 does not exist in Title 18.

- The responsibility to quash dissent has been transferred (apparently) to the Puerto Rico government. The Board no longer has authority to enforce the law against strikes or lockouts by public employees, but may "ensure the prompt enforcement."[11]
- A new paragraph declares acceptable to the Board any voluntary agreement reached by the Puerto Rico government with creditors before the enactment of the Act.
- Puerto Rico government employees are not subject to the $1,000 fine for providing false information to the Board (remember that originally they would be subject to one year of jail, and the F1 eliminated the jail penalty, but not the fine). Now they will be subject to the Penal Code of Puerto Rico.
- The Federal Court of the District of Columbia, as well as the Court of Appeals for the District of Columbia were eliminated as the courts with jurisdiction. Now it will be the District of Puerto Rico. The extreme limitation on filing petitions before the U.S. Supreme Court (which the F1 had set to 10 days from 90), was eliminated.
- Adds a requirement that the Board work with the Puerto Rico Comptroller's office to keep a registry of all contracts executed by the Puerto Rico government.

This bill does not require that the contracts executed by the Board be made public.

- The Board is granted the authority to approve "certain contracts," which are not defined. It also includes a section where Congress informs that it "is its sense" that the intervention of the Board in contracting processes is to make it more effective, increase public faith in the contracting process, and avoid additional bureaucracy.[12]

"Increase public faith in the contracting process" when the Board's contracts are secret? Really?

- A new provision prohibits the Board to impede compliance with federal consent decrees or programs.
- The Board may make recommendations directly to Congress to change federal laws or rules, or for the Federal government to take actions that may help Puerto Rico comply with the Fiscal Plan. It doesn't have to go through the President, as it was under the F1.
- The Board must also provide the U.S. President, Congress, the Governor, and the Legislature with a report on the use of its budget and the gifts it received.
- Eliminated the control that the F1 had granted the Board over the tax exemption agreements. It also

added a prohibition to the Board to disclose any information provided by the Governor to the Board regarding the tax exemption agreements.

I suspect the multinationals and pharmas had something to do with this change.

- As to the other territories of the U.S., Congress added a requirement that a Board would be put in place for them only if their Legislature adopts a law requiring the Board. Of course, as befits the territorial clause, in another section, Congress reserves the right to impose one if it thinks it should.

## Board Funding

- The authorization of the Board to issue bonds to fund its operations is eliminated.
- So is the appropriation of Congress to pay for the professionals needed.

## Term of the Board

- The provisions in the F1 that provided for the Board to keep supervising the budgeting process forever were eliminated.
- Now there must be balanced budgets for four consecutive years instead of five, for the Board to cease operating.

These changes are not enough to make the F2 less "colonialist" than the F1. And the rest of the changes made in the F2 neutralize these changes to the Board.

## Approval Process of Fiscal Plans and Budgets

These sections were amended to make them clearer, since the section in the F1 for the approval of the Fiscal Plan was almost unintelligible.

- The F2 requires that the Governor provide a Fiscal Plan of at least five years. The Fiscal Plan's purpose is to "provide a method to achieve fiscal responsibility and access to the capital markets."[13] Among the new requirements for a Fiscal Plan are:
  - include a debt sustainability analysis
  - provide for capital expenditures and investments necessary to promote economic growth
  - to the greatest extent feasible, adopt recommendations submitted to the Puerto Rico government by the Board
- Eliminates the requirement that Congress and the U.S. President be notified if the Fiscal Plan and the budgets are prepared by consensus among the Governor, the Legislature, and the Board.
- Now it is the Board who will prepare the revenue forecasts for the budgets, not the Governor and the Legislature, as it was in the F1.

- It provides for separate budgets for instrumentalities and the central government. Unless the Board decides that it will want to supervise and approve an instrumentality's budget, it will not have to be submitted to the Board for approval. This applies only if the instrumentality's budget does not have to be submitted to the Governor for approval.

My guess? This was done to protect PREPA's creditors and the negotiation from the Board's messing up their budgets and agreements.

Two comments:

I find the debt sustainability analysis requirement the most interesting. The foremost experts on these analyses are in the International Monetary Fund (and even they get it wrong sometimes; look at what they did to Greece). Who will prepare the analysis required in this Fiscal Plan? From where will these experts come? Former IMF employees? IMF employees by a petition of the U.S.'s government to the benefit of its subnational jurisdiction, Puerto Rico?

In the F1, the Board could decide, unilaterally by the vote of three non-elected persons, to implement any change to Puerto Rico laws, rules, regulations, court opinions, operations and anything that they, in their sole discretion, thought was a good idea. This version eliminates that provision. But, the roundabout is this new requirement that the Fiscal Plan has, to the greatest extent feasible, to adopt recommendations submitted to the Puerto Rico government by the Board. What do you think will happen?

If the Puerto Rico government does not approve the recommendation that the Board wants to implement, the Board will not approve either the Fiscal Plan or the Budget. It would certainly not approve a restructuring certification.

No matter what the U.S. Congress may say, the absolute power over Puerto Rico's government and public policy did not change at all.

## Vieques, the Intriguing Transfer

The F2 eliminates the provision that the transfer of land to Puerto Rico could be transferred forward. However, it adds a restriction as to the purpose, although the bill has a mistake and is so badly drafted, that there is no way to know for which purpose Puerto Rico can use the transferred land.

## Wages Stay Down ... Forever

F1 permanently depressed the minimum wage for every Puerto Rican by authorizing an hourly wage of $4.25 to workers younger than 25, and making unenforceable in Puerto Rico the Department of Labor 2015 regulations that update overtime regulations.

As to younger workers, F2 keeps the authorization to pay $4.25, but now requires that the Governor designate a period of no more than five years during which this depressed wage would apply.

The decision, as expected, is subject to the Board's approval.

The F2 limits the wage depression of young workers to five years, but keeps the provision that declares the new regulations on overtime unenforceable in Puerto Rico. So, wages for Puerto Ricans are still depressed by decision of the U.S. Congress.

[7]

# Simplicity Is not the Way They Go

THIS CHAPTER WILL DISCUSS the changes the F2 made to the provisions related to the stay on litigation, the fast-track privatization process, and the debt restructuring.

## THE STAY ON LITIGATION

- The stay is reduced from 18 months to ten, with a specific end date: 15 February 2017.
- Clarifies that the stay does not apply to the implementation of any "restructuring support agreement" executed by the government by the time the Act is enacted.

This is for PREPA's agreement.

## The Czar

Since this title was the most beneficial to the investors' interests, it changed very little. And the changes were to make the fast-track even faster:

- The Board must provide the governor with the names of the candidates to privatization czar within 60 days after the appointment of four members.
- The Revitalization Coordinator may be removed without cause.
- Now the czar stays in place until the critical projects are completed, and not only while the Board is operating, as in the F1.

So Puerto Rico may be without the Board, but keep the czar.

- Adds that petitions to consider a project a critical project can be submitted only while the Board is in operation.

They had to include this provision, since under the F2 there may be a Coordinator without a Board.

- F2 adds a requirement to the proposals for energy critical projects: now proponents must address how the critical project will "lower energy costs for rate payers and increase availability of affordable energy."[1]

- The process of evaluating the proposals was clarified, and the F2 requires that the Revitalization Coordinator consult with the Governor, and make the Governor's recommendation part of its report.
- Adds the requirement that if the proposed project will connect to the transmission or distribution systems of PREPA, the Energy Commission must provide a recommendation.
- Adopts a requirement that the critical projects be prioritized in every government agency.
- Adds that all reports and justifications on each project proposal be made public within five days after the analysis is completed.
- The Federal court in Puerto Rico does not have exclusive jurisdiction anymore.

## A New Report

The F2 incorporates a section that amends the Consolidated and Further Continuing Appropriations Act of 2015.[2] This Act required that, as to the "insular areas" (definition that includes Puerto Rico), the Secretary of the U.S. Department of the Interior prepared an "energy action plan" to address the energy needs of Puerto Rico, and assisted Puerto Rico in implementing the plan.[3] Originally, the plan had to have been developed by June 2015.

This "energy action plan" had to include:

1. Recommendations, based on the comprehensive energy plan (where applicable), to:

   a. reduce reliance and expenditures on fuel shipped to Puerto Rico from ports outside the United States
   b. develop and utilize domestic fuel energy sources
   c. improve performance of energy infrastructure and overall energy efficiency
2. A schedule for implementation of such recommendations and identification and prioritization of specific projects.
3. A financial and engineering plan for implementing and sustaining projects.
4. Benchmarks for measuring progress toward implementation.[4]

The comprehensive energy plan emphasizes "indigenous renewable sources of energy" so that reliance on energy imports can be minimized.

The F2 amends the Consolidated and Further Continuing Appropriations Act by:

- extending the plan development to 180 days after the PROMESA is enacted
- transferring the responsibility of preparing the report to the U.S. Secretary of the Department of Energy.

There was no reason to include Puerto Rico in the definition of insular area nor require the Secretary of the Interior to prepare the report: The Department of the Interior has no jurisdiction over Puerto Rico.

## Restructuring

The rational process of the F1 was gutted. The changes in the F2 are:

- If the Board believes that the federal court in Puerto Rico will not provide proper case management of the restructuring petitions, it may present the petition in the district court where it has any of its offices.

New York! New York!

- Adds three new requirements before the Board may issue a restructuring certificate.
- Increases to five the number of members of the Board who must approve a petition for a restructuring certification.
- Eliminates the authorization for the Board to file joint petitions and plans of adjustment for affiliated debtors.
- Only the debtor may file a plan of adjustment and its modifications — in F1 it was the Board.
- Adds a collective action clause of two-thirds of bondholders for each pool of bonds:
  - each issuer must have at least one pool
  - bonds secured by a lien on property will be a pool
  - pools will be established by priority or security, seniority, guarantees, and revenue streams

- modifications may be made if at least two-thirds of the outstanding principal amount of the bonds in the pool vote in favor
- before taking the proposed modification to a vote, each issuer must consult with the pool that will be affected by the modification

Collective Action Clauses authorize the amendment of payment terms of a bond issue if a majority (or supermajority) of bondholders agree. There are three major types of CACs: (1) in a majority by series, there must be a vote by bond series, and the restructuring for each series can proceed if a majority in each series agrees; (2) in a two-tier aggregated majority, there must be a majority by series and a majority of all bonds outstanding in the aggregate; (3) a single-tier aggregated majority binds all bondholders if a majority of all bonds outstanding in the aggregate are in favor of the restructuring. In F2, the CAC is a majority by series (each pool).

- The requirement that the federal judge certify all issues of Puerto Rico law to the Puerto Rico Supreme Court was eliminated.

My comments:

I expect federal judges that could be from a Federal court in any district, and who may know nothing about civil law, interpreting Puerto Rico law. This is because the certification of Puerto Rico law to the Puerto Rico Supreme Court is related to the doctrine of abstention of the federal courts. It was much easier and cost-effective for every litigant if the requirement to certify was obligatory.

Now, the certification may very well be object of litigation, as part of a petition for the Federal court to abstain from deciding a case. The petition would be filed because 95% of Puerto Rico debt is issued under Puerto Rico law. The mandatory certification took care of any argument in favor of abstention.

There could be the remote possibility that this may also be interpreted as a way to force litigants to the Puerto Rico courts, because practically all restructuring must be made under Puerto Rico law and the Puerto Rico Supreme Court has never interpreted any of those provisions.

> But, as you have deduced, my skepticism is very high, so I find it quite difficult to believe this is the reason. I believe the purpose is to have New York federal judges interpreting Puerto Rico law, even if for the first time.
>
> I wonder: who do creditors believe they could get as their judge? The one who favored Argentina's creditors and who upended the world's sovereign debt market?

## New Meaningless Provisions

There is a new paragraph on the findings of Congress as to the causes of the crisis that repeats the same reasons of fiscal mismanagement, inefficiencies, and excessive borrowing. Of course, nothing as to the economic contraction, the constraints facing Puerto Rico in a global economy, or the high production costs because of the "burdensome federal regulatory policy."

Congress keeps insisting that to create economic growth it is enough to use an approach to fiscal, management and structural problems that "exempts no part of the Puerto Rico government," is under "federal statutory authority," and that may restructure debt.[5]

> But, I add, that provide nothing for economic development.

Another new paragraph on the purposes of the bill repeats the same reasons, and adds this subparagraph that says nothing, and says a lot. In my opinion, the best paragraph in all of this F2:

> ...benefit the lives of 3.5 million American citizens living in Puerto Rico by encouraging the Government of Puerto Rico to resolve its long-standing fiscal issues governance issues and return to economic growth.[6]

Isn't it wonderful, this language?

> I would love to know how is it that resolving fiscal issues, without further ado, returns Puerto Rico to economic growth. If the U.S. Congress knows, why won't it tell me?

## Back to the Future

In practice, this version loosens microscopically the control that the F1 had given the Board over the Puerto Rico government. However, the Board still has ultimate power over the government and public policy, so it will be very difficult for the Board to evade the responsibility for results. Is that what they want?

> It is true that the U.S. Congress made sure that any and every harm that resulted from the decisions taken by the Board would be paid by the Puerto Rico Government (see Chapter 1). Is the Board going to use the plenary control the U.S. Congress is gifting it and not accept responsibility for the mistakes it will make?

And this disagreeable process has also made obvious the biggest issue of all: the need to change Puerto Rico's political status. The U.S., even if it wants to deny it, has historically subsidized sectors of Puerto Rico's economy, because that is what colonial powers must do with their colonial economies, since it extracts plenty of money from the unsubsidized sectors. Just one example, as this is not the topic of the book: Puerto Rico has the equivalent of less than 1% of the U.S. population, yet generates 25% of the revenues reported by the U.S. merchant marine industry.[7]

Colonial economies respond to the needs of the metropolis — that's what is called mercantilism. That is why Puerto Rico has today very few productive sectors, and the diversified, export-driven economy that it was when the U.S. invaded Puerto Rico has been limited to one industry: pharmaceuticals.

If the U.S. does not want to subsidize any sector of Puerto Rico's economy then it should be prepared to open the political status debate so Puerto Rico can have the tools it needs to compete in today's global economy.

Open the debate in a serious manner, without persecuting the proponents and defenders of any status acceptable to the international community, as the U.S. has done against Puerto Rican *independentistas* since it invaded Puerto Rico in 1898.

> Using the bogeyman of "bailouts" does not solve the problem. It breeds bigotry and hatred, but gets no one any closer to a solution.

If the U.S. insists in keeping the shackles on Puerto Rico and its economy in a cage, this bill is just the latest chapter of the saga and most definitely not the end.

[8]

# Excuses, Excuses

THE PROMESA'S NEW ITERATION is still being renegotiated in the U.S. Congress. According to news reports, they expect it to be ready by June or July.

That timetable certainly complicates matters: on 1 July 2016 there are total payments due on various bond issues of over $2 billion. Puerto Rico does not have the money to pay. Such a default would be the biggest in the municipal credit market in the U.S. and its ripple effects cannot be completely foreseen. Although I would expect the federal regulators to have been prepared for this eventuality for a while. Especially since some analysts have been expecting it for years.

The reasons given by the Members of Congress for the opposition to the approval of a debt restructuring mechanism for Puerto Rico are two:

1. the retroactive application of the restructuring — which is nonsense, since:

  a. all bankruptcy laws approved by the U.S. Congress have been applied retroactively
  b. the U.S. Supreme Court has declared such application legal, and
  c. all bankruptcy laws applied to Puerto Rico until the inexplicable and unexplained exclusion in 1984
2. that such a restructuring would set a precedent for the states, particularly Illinois — more nonsense, since:
  a. the states are states and Puerto Rico is a territory, and
  b. territories are subject to the despotic territorial clause, that applies only to territories and not to states

Let's discuss these two objections in more detail.

## Retroactive Bankruptcy

Every bankruptcy law enacted by the U.S. Congress, since the first one in 1800, has been applied retroactively, that is, to loans granted before there was a bankruptcy law.

> For over 200 years the bankruptcy practice and precedent in the U.S. has been to subject all creditor claims to bankruptcy, independently of when the loans were granted.

Why, then, are some Members of Congress so aghast about the implementation of a debt restructuring process for Puerto Rico debt?

Ever since the first federal municipality bankruptcy law was enacted in the U.S. in 1934, and until the unexplained prohibition of 1984, Puerto Rico municipalities could file for bankruptcy under the U.S. Bankruptcy Code.

It was not until 1984 when Congress, thru language inserted by Senator Strom Thurmond, without any public discussion or explanation for the record, prohibited bankruptcy filing for Puerto Rico's municipalities.

And just as what Congress giveth Congress taketh away, what Congress taketh away it may giveth again.

## A Little History

The argument used by these Members of Congress ignores U.S. Supreme Court precedent, U.S. centuries-old bankruptcy practice, and is an argument for limiting Congress's powers over enacting bankruptcy laws in the U.S.

> It is also a call for a despotic expansion of Congressional rule over Puerto Rico.

I'll explain.

Federal bankruptcy laws in the U.S. have always been applied retroactively, beginning with the first one enacted in 1800. That was done by necessity, since all of them, until the Bankruptcy Code of 1978, were enacted in response to major financial disasters. The 1841 Bankruptcy Act was the first to provide for the voluntary filing by a debtor, and it applied to all persons owing debt.

The first municipal bankruptcy legislation was enacted in 1934 during the Great Depression, revised in 1937 and upheld by the Supreme Court in 1938 — and it applied to existing debt.

## What the U.S. Supreme Court Has Said

In 1982 the U.S. Supreme Court agreed with the argument that the authority granted to Congress under the Bankruptcy Clause "has been regularly construed to authorize the retrospective impairment of contractual obligations," citing a 1902 case.[1]

The matter of retroactivity had been considered by lower courts before, and:

> the decisions of the lower federal courts generally indicated that the retroactive feature of the amendments was not constitutionally problematic, on the ground that the bankruptcy power necessarily entails the power retroactively to impair contractual obligations and related liens.[2]

The Supreme Court has held that there is no constitutional prohibition for approving retroactive federal bankruptcy laws that impaired contractual rights, since the prohibition of the Contract Clause of the Constitution applies only to laws enacted by the states. Therefore, there is no constitutional prohibition for approving a federal bankruptcy law that applies to debt issued before the law was enacted.

For over 200 years bankruptcy legislation has been applied retroactively. For at least 170 years bankruptcy legislation has been retroactively applied to creditors of a debtor voluntarily filing a bankruptcy petition.

As to municipalities, bankruptcy applicability has been retroactive for 77 years: ever since it was first enacted, when it applied to Puerto Rico municipalities.

## The Reasons

The purpose of these absurd arguments on retroactive bankruptcy, that go against historical application and legal precedent, is that someone (meaning, of course, Puerto Rico) makes up to creditors the losses they suffered in other Chapter 9 bankruptcies. That is the reason that for all intents and purposes investors' representative told Congress in a hearing on 26 February 2015.[3]

The written testimony of their representative[4] states that "Chapter 9 hurts bondholders", and details "how badly" they were hurt in the bankruptcies of Detroit, Stockton, Vallejo, and Jefferson County. The oral testimony repeated the argument, and buttressed the idea of the surprise, ignoring decades of judicial precedent and centuries of U.S. bankruptcy practice.

> It is not difficult to conclude why these declarations about losses on prior bankruptcies are being made.

## A Precedent for the 50 States

The second reason presented by the U.S. Congress is that decisions on Puerto Rico, which are taken under the plenary power of the territorial clause, may set precedents for the states.

> It seems the plenary power of the territorial clause is so all-encompassing, that it covers not only the territories, but also the 50 states.

I've been told that having a precedent would help in preempting any excuse that "it has never been done before."

Which is true. But still does not explain how the same Congress that declares being worried about any precedent-setting for the 50 states under the territorial clause, ignores clear precedent under the bankruptcy clause because it doesn't suit its current interests.

Generally speaking, I do not think there is need to base a solution on precedents, because of:

- the nature of Congress's plenary power over Puerto Rico
- the nature of the territorial clause
- the interpretations by the U.S. Supreme Court

### The Territorial Clause

Section 3 of Article IV of the U.S. Constitution reads:

> The Congress shall have Power to dispose of and make all needful Rules and Regulations respecting the Territory or other Property belonging to the United

> States; and nothing in this Constitution shall be so construed as to Prejudice any Claims of the United States, or of any particular State.

When Spain ceded Puerto Rico to the U.S. under the Paris Peace Treaty of 1898 that put an end to the Spanish-American War, the legal status of Puerto Rico within the U.S. was undefined.[5]

The U.S. had been interested in the control of Puerto Rico because of its unparalleled geographical location that gave the U.S. great commercial and military advantages.

It wasn't until 1901 in the first of a series of decisions by the U.S. Supreme Court that the legal status of Puerto Rico and Puerto Ricans was determined. These series of cases are called the Insular Cases.[6]

In these cases, the U.S. Supreme Court decided that Puerto Rico was a territory subject to the territorial clause. It came up with a new category of "territory" that differed from all the other territories with which the U.S. had dealt with in its unrelenting expansion to the west: what the Supreme Court called an "unincorporated territory."

The Court considered Puerto Rico a territory whose inhabitants were so different from the U.S. population that it could not be welcomed into the U.S. In practical terms, that it could not be on the path to statehood.

However, since the U.S. had acquired Puerto Rico through war, the U.S. Supreme Court considered it was not prudent for it to limit the powers that the Executive and

Legislative Branches should have in their administration and control of this territory.

This eventually gave rise to the theory that Puerto Rico "belongs to the U.S. but is not part of the U.S."

Not even the collective naturalization of Puerto Ricans in 1917 changed the U.S. Supreme Court's conclusion. The Court actually ended up holding that Puerto Ricans could be treated differently than the other U.S. citizens, because we live in a territory that could be treated differently.

> Think about it. It is the same legal theory used for the serfs in the Middle Ages: our rights depend on what part of the U.S. we are on. As soon as Puerto Ricans move to the U.S. we have rights that we do not have while we live in Puerto Rico — rights that flow from the U.S. citizenship the U.S. Congress unilaterally imposed upon us in 1917. Rights that disappear if we are standing on Puerto Rico soil.

This different treatment is a consequence of what the Court held was the plenary power the U.S. Congress has over territories, based on the expansive language of the territorial clause.

## No Similarities

This is a very general summary of the conundrum that Puerto Rico's political status and the legal rights of Puerto Ricans represent to the U.S.

But even as general as it is, it is clear that the legal provisions that rule Puerto Rico's place in the U.S. constitutional order are very different than the rights and rules that apply to a state.

A state in a federated country is considered a cosovereign with the federal government. The federal government has the rights the states have ceded the federal government, and no more.

Puerto Rico is a sub-sovereign. It is lower in hierarchy than the federal government, and even than the cosovereigns. Under the legal precedent set by the U.S. Supreme Court, Puerto Rico has no power to cede but, to the contrary, only has the very limited power its metropolis, through the U.S. Congress, has deigned to grant it.

> For a decision taken under the territorial clause to be applicable to one of the 50 states, the state must have voluntarily decided to keep Puerto Rico company and subject itself to the ignominy of the plenary power of the territorial clause.
>
> The argument bandied about by the Members of Congress is so absurd it's embarrassing.

# [PART 3]

## Version of 18 May 2016

[9]

# A Little Bit of Marketing

THE FOURTH DRAFT OF the PROMESA[1] has a new bill number, H.R. 5278, and six major changes from the version of 12 April:

1. Changes (again!) how the Members of the Board are selected.
2. Requires the Government Accountability Office (GAO) to issue a report on the Small Business Administration programs in Puerto Rico.
3. Requires the GAO to issue a report on whether the regulation on overtime pay would negatively affect Puerto Rico's economy before the regulations are enforceable by Puerto Rican workers.
4. Creates a Congressional task force on changes needed to U.S. laws and regulations that "impede" Puerto Rico's economic development.
5. Changes (again!) how long the privatization czar's office will be in place.

6. Overhauls the definitions and voting requirements on creditor collective action clauses (CACs).

It seems the U.S. Congress cannot make up its mind on how to select the persons that will bypass Puerto Rico's elected officials and its Constitution.

The Members of the Board must be willing to follow the path dictated by Congress and the interests that Congress is defending, but not be so offensive in its purpose as to raise issues of colonialism.

After all, colonialism is one of the "worries" the third draft of the bill, H.R. 4900, tried to correct.

This version follows the path of the prior ones in which Puerto Rico's government is co-opted by persons named by the U.S. President with no input or participation from Puerto Ricans. It follows once again the government-from-outside style established by the Foraker Act of 1900, so I will refer to this version as F3.

> I will compare this version dated 10:58 p.m. 18 May 2016 (F3) to the version dated 12 April 2016 to which I referred as F2 in Chapters 6 and 7. If necessary, I will also compare it to the F1, the draft dated 29 March 2016 that I analyzed in Chapters 1 through 5.

## The Missing Chaos

The summary[2] of this version of the bill and of the "key refinements"[3] made by the F3 repeat the language they use in the prior versions regarding the causes for the fiscal, economic, and financial crisis in Puerto Rico — that according to the U.S. Congress stem exclusively from Puerto Rico.

The summary mentions once again the need to institute reforms to promote economic growth, but they are framed by the requirement that Puerto Rico meet all its credit obligations.

The U.S. Congress states in this F3 that the bill will "bring lawful order to chaos in Puerto Rico" and that it will "institute fiscal and economic reforms to promote growth and ensure the Island meets its credit obligations."[4]

Congress even dares state that the bill "will restore the rule of law and protect the lawful rights of the Island's investors."[5]

> The language about the "chaos" and the "unlawfulness" that according to the U.S. Congress prevails in Puerto Rico reminds me that when you repeat a lie enough times, people will eventually start to believe it.

## THE SOLEMN DUTY

Many Republican Members of the U.S. Congress have been saying for months that any bill providing for the restructuring of debt issued by the Puerto Rico government would be a bailout — a costly bailout — for U.S. taxpayers. They mean, of course, taxpayers living in the United States and not the "U.S. citizens living in Puerto Rico," who also pay U.S. taxes.

> This is the first version of the bill in which the U.S. Congress goes all-out in its desire to remind Puerto Rico and all Puerto Ricans that we are subject to the plenary powers of the U.S. Congress and that we have no sovereignty whatsoever except the scraps that Congress deigns to throw our way.

There are two cases pending before the United States Supreme Court that deal precisely with how much sovereignty Puerto Rico has regarding its debts and its internal affairs. The cases bring to the forefront the representations that the United States made to Puerto Rico and to the United Nations regarding Puerto Rico's autonomy after 1952 and the enactment of its Constitution.

The Supreme Court could hold either that:

- the representations made really have no effect whatsoever on Puerto Rico's self-government (which means that the United States lied regarding Puerto Rico's degree of autonomy both to us Puerto Ricans and to the international community), or
- the changes enacted and agreed upon by the U.S. Congress and the Puerto Rico's government in 1952 indeed created a new relationship between Puerto Rico and the United States that excludes Puerto Rico from the territorial clause.

> I believe that the U.S. Supreme Court will hold[6] that Puerto Rico is still subject to the territorial clause and to the plenary powers of the U.S. Congress.

However, Congress is hedging its bets. This F3 mentions more often than the prior versions the subjugation of Puerto Rico to the U.S. Congress under the territorial clause and, as we will see, ties the authorization to restructure debt to the existence of the Board.

I suppose this language is trying to anticipate the possibility that the U.S. Supreme Court will hold the United States to the representations it made to Puerto Rico and to the United Nations. It is also a message to the organizations in Puerto Rico that have announced a legal challenge to the Board as a violation of U.S. Public Laws 81-600[7] and 82-447,[8] which authorized a Constitutional government for Puerto Rico.

Remember that every jurisdiction under the United States (except for the territories) is entitled to the protection of Chapter 9 of the U.S. Bankruptcy Code. To compare granting Puerto Rico issuers access to Chapter 9 to a bailout is nonsense. That is the U.S. Congress for you.

But to prove that Congress takes seriously Puerto Rico's condition as a territory, it has added this language to the bill's summary:

> The federal government is the sovereign for all territories and as such it carries a solemn responsibility to help Puerto Rico resolve its fiscal problems.

> I need to see the dictionary used by the drafters of the bill. Not one of the dictionaries and thesauruses in my library has a definition that would make the PROMESA "solemn."

## That Unfair, Abusive, Awful Chapter 9

The F3 takes great pains in distinguishing the protection granted to U.S. government issuers under Chapter 9 of the U.S. Bankruptcy Code from the limited debt restructuring apparently granted to Puerto Rico issuers.

In its zeal to justify their refusal in recognizing Puerto Rico's right to debt restructuring and their interest to treat Puerto Rico differently, the drafters of the bill directly attack Chapter 9 as an unfair law for creditors that lets issuers run amok.[9]

They again use Detroit as an example of the awfulness of Chapter 9. This is unsurprising since this is the language that some Puerto Rico creditors use in their lobbying to block any possibility for Puerto Rico to restructure its debt. And these lobbyists have been quite productive and effective.

> What I wonder is this: if these Members of the U.S. Congress believe Chapter 9 of the U.S. Bankruptcy Code is such an awful piece of legislation, why haven't they filed a bill to amend it?

## THE STATES AS TERRITORIES

The F3 finally puts paid to the idiocy repeated for the last six months that a restructuring procedure enacted under the territorial clause would set a precedent to the 50 states of the U.S.

It is here that the U.S. Congress publicly admits that the application of the bill to any state would violate the Tenth Amendment of the U.S. Constitution that recognizes the sovereignty of each of the 50 states within the federal system of government:

> The powers not delegated to the United States by the Constitution, nor prohibited by it to the states, are reserved to the states respectively, or to the people.

To make it very clear that no state can ever benefit from this restructuring procedure, the summary refers to the bill's instruction that the law be codified under the title of the U.S. Code that refers to territories. And to end the discussion (which Members of Congress fanned, but maybe they believe no one remembers), the bill's summary proclaims that:

> If a state wanted to use the Act as a precedent, they would need to revoke their status as a state, become a U.S. territory and petition the U.S. government for an Oversight Board to be eligible.[10]

Took the U.S. Congress long enough.

## The New Sponsors

The F3 adds two sponsors to the bill: original sponsor Sean P. Duffy (Wisconsin) is joined by Rob Bishop (Utah) and F. James Sensenbrenner (Wisconsin). All Republicans.

[10]

# Metropolis Likes Reports

IN ITS AMENDMENTS, THE F3 requires that four reports be prepared and submitted to the U.S. Congress. These reports are to be prepared by the U.S. government on:

1. How the U.S. government programs for small businesses work in Puerto Rico.
2. What is the impact of federal laws, rules, and regulations on Puerto Rico's economic development.
3. What is the impact that the new regulations issued by the U.S. Secretary of Labor on overtime would have on the economy of Puerto Rico.
4. Whether the U.S. Bureau of the Census should expand data collection to Puerto Rico as to the labor force statistics.

## The GAO on the HUBZone

Within 180 days from the enactment of the bill the Government Accounting Office must submit a report

> on the application and utilization of contracting activities of the Administration (including contracting activities relating to HUBZone small business concerns) in Puerto Rico. The report shall also identify any provisions of Federal law that may create an obstacle to the efficient implementation of such contracting activities.[1]

### The HUBZone

The HUBZone[2] is a program of the U.S. Small Business Administration (SBA) to help small businesses have preferential access to federal public procurement opportunities. The goal of the Federal government is to award 3% of federal prime contracts to HUBZone-certified small business concerns.

The Historically Underutilized Business Zones (HUBZone) program's purpose is to promote economic development and growth in distressed areas, which are designated by the SBA as having been historically underutilized by businesses.

The law establishes how the data gathered by the SBA will be used to determine whether a zone is designated as a HUBZone.

Among the information gathered by the SBA is data from the U.S. Bureau of Labor Statistics, the Department of

Defense, the Department of Housing and Urban Development, and the U.S. Census Bureau.

According to the information gathered by the SBA a HUBZone can be designated as one of four types:

- qualified census tract
- qualified nonmetropolitan county
- qualified Indian reservation
- qualified base closure area

Puerto Rico's HUBZones are classified under the qualified base closure area, qualified census tract, or qualified nonmetropolitan county.

> Puerto Rico's small businesses do not typically participate in the procurement process of the Federal government; such a report could be helpful in identifying why.

## THE TASK FORCE

The F3 provides for the establishment of a Task Force within the legislative branch of the U.S. government, called the Congressional Task Force on Economic Growth in Puerto Rico.

> Since the purpose of the Board is to "provide a method for a covered territory to achieve fiscal responsibility and access to the capital markets,"[3] I am surprised that the fourth draft of the PROMESA includes a section attempting to identify the impediments the U.S.

imposes on Puerto Rico that bar us from developing our economy in the medium and long term.

## The Report

By 31 December 2016 the Task Force must issue a report regarding:

- "impediments in current Federal law and programs to economic growth in Puerto Rico"
- changes to Federal law and programs that "would serve to spur sustainable long-term economic growth, job creation and attract investment in Puerto Rico"
- other appropriate additional information[4]

The U.S. trade treaties are a key factor in Puerto Rico's impossibility to participate in the global markets and benefit from the global economy. All U.S. trade treaties apply to Puerto Rico, many of them explicitly by requirement of the U.S. counterparties.

Although treaties are U.S. law, I doubt very much that the Task Force will refer in its report to the disastrous impact the U.S. free trade treaties have had on Puerto Rico. That issue goes directly to the political status, which shall not be discussed.

The bill states that "to the greatest extent practicable" the report should reflect the "shared views of all eight members, except that the report may contain dissenting views."

## THE MEMBERS

The Task Force will be composed of eight members, equally divided by chamber and political party:

- two members of the House of Representatives shall be appointed by the Speaker of the House (Republican)
- two members of the House of Representatives shall be appointed by the Minority Leader of the House (Democrat)
- two members of the Senate shall be appointed by the Majority Leader of the Senate (Republican)
- two members of the Senate shall be appointed by the Minority Leader of the Senate (Democrat).

In all cases the appointments must be made in coordination with the Committee on Natural Resources of the House, and the Committee on Energy and Natural Resources of the Senate.

> These are the committees of the U.S. Congress that have original jurisdiction over Puerto Rico.

The appointments must be made within 30 days of the enactment of the bill, and the chair of the Task Force shall be designated by the Speaker of the House.

The F3 requires that the Task Force consult with the:

- Puerto Rico Legislative Assembly
- Puerto Rico Department of Economic Development and Commerce
- Puerto Rico's private sector.

Unlike the Board, the Task Force shall use existing facilities, services, and staff of the U.S. Congress, although no additional funds will be appropriated for this purpose.

Once the report is submitted, the Task Force shall terminate.

> As you may imagine, I expect no implementable report.
>
> An honest discussion of the "impediments in current Federal law" on Puerto Rico's economic development will, by necessity, paint a very unflattering and despotic picture of the real effects of the U.S. Congress's plenary powers under the U.S. Constitution's Territorial Clause.
>
> No member of Congress will flat-out admit that the political status is drowning Puerto Rico, killing its opportunities of participating in the global economy, and prohibiting any serious approach to foreign investors and partners.
>
> I expect a report that will conclude that some federal regulations could be an "impediment," but not to such an extent that Federal law has to be revised.
>
> And I expect that the Task Force's first conclusion will be that the main "impediment" is the Puerto Ricans' right to earn a decent wage.

## THE GAO ON THE LIVABLE WAGE

This F3 adds two requirements (one of them a report by the GAO) before the 2015 overtime regulations apply to Puerto Rico. The F2 had blocked the application of the regulations to Puerto Rican workers forever. The requirements added by the F3 are that:

1. The GAO, within two years after the enactment of the PROMESA, shall

> examine the economic conditions in Puerto Rico and shall transmit a report to Congress assessing the impact of applying the [overtime regulations] to Puerto Rico, taking into consideration regional, metropolitan, and non-metropolitan salary and cost-of-living differences.[5]

2. The Secretary of Labor, after considering the GAO report, provide a written determination to Congress that applying the 2015 overtime regulations to Puerto Rico would not have a negative impact on the economy of Puerto Rico.

Considering the language, it seems no other action would be necessary by the U.S. Congress. If the Secretary of Labor determines that the regulations will not impact negatively the economy of Puerto Rico, the regulations will have force and effect in Puerto Rico.

This is the only instance in which a U.S. government agency must make a finding that a Federal regulation will not impact Puerto Rico negatively before it applies to Puerto Rico.

> This should be the policy for all federal laws and regulations. But that is not the case: all laws, rules, and regulations of the U.S. government automatically apply to Puerto Rico, irrespective of the impact it may have on its economy.[6]
>
> The only exception is made for the regulations concerning wages. I wonder why?

Also, the U.S. Congress changes again the amendments that it wants to make to the Fair Labor Standards Act of 1938.

- Instead of amending a paragraph that also applied to other jurisdictions, Congress will now add a paragraph that applies only to Puerto Rico. F3 maintains the authority of the Governor to approve a wage of $4.25, but lowers it to four years instead of the five years provided in the F2.
- This draft eliminates the specific reference to $4.25 that it had included in F2 and goes back to reference paragraph (1).

> It eliminates the imposition of a minimum wage exclusive for Puerto Rico since if the wage of $4.25 changes for any of the other jurisdictions, it would change for Puerto Rican workers too (hopefully to increase).

- Prohibits that the term designated by the Governor extend beyond the termination of the Board.

## Labor Force Statistics

F3 includes a "sense of Congress" that the Bureau of the Census should issue a feasibility study to expand data collection to Puerto Rico related to the labor force statistics. The bill suggests that the Bureau request the funding needed to conduct the study as part of its budget for fiscal year 2018.

> "Sense of Congress" provisions are used for Congress to send a message or state an opinion, but are not enforceable provisions of the law.
>
> The data collection for the Puerto Rico labor force statistics is designed and conducted by the Puerto Rico government. This provision wants the Bureau of the Census to study the feasibility of its taking over this data collection, but does not require it.

## The Business of Electricity

The submittal date of the "energy action plan" that the F2 required the U.S. Secretary of Energy to prepare "addressing the energy needs" of Puerto Rico has been extended by 90 days: from 180 to 270.

[11]

# Metropolis Loves Control

THE CHANGES IN THE F3 that I will discuss in this Chapter are:

- the selection of the Board's members
- the process of approving Fiscal Plans and budgets.

## THE BOARD

The F3 reflects the trouble the U.S. Congress is having in deciding how to select the members of the Board. The process must appear rational, but also make sure that the selected persons will implement the purpose of the law: that the creditors that have spent so much money in lobbying get the results they want.

> Austerity is the name of the game, even if it has accomplished exactly nothing in every country in which it has been implemented.

On the other hand, a Board that controls all moneys, revenues, expenses, budgets, fiscal plans, privatizations, laws, rules, regulations, public policy on employment, economic growth, health, education, etc., has nowhere to hide from the consequences of its decisions and policies.

> Not even the International Monetary Fund has been able to hide from the mess it created in Greece.

For all the years that the Board is in place, anything and everything that the Puerto Rico government does is subject to the Board's review and approval. It will be impossible for the Board to refuse to accept responsibility for the consequences of their "reviews," "approvals," and "certifications."

> I too would be very worried about how to select the members of the Board who will run the Puerto Rico government and will be solely responsible for the result. The U.S. Congress has justified its takeover of the Puerto Rico government by stating that we Puerto Ricans have done everything wrong and that the Board will save the "U.S. citizens living in Puerto Rico" from ourselves.
>
> What an embarrassment it will be if these saviors are incapable of turning the boat around.

These are the changes from the F2 to the F3:

- The Puerto Rico Governor is no longer an ex officio Member of the Board.

- The F3 deleted the provisions on how to choose the Board's Chair, as well as the provisions on term of service and removal of the Members.

Most probably this change is a mistake that will be fixed in the next draft.

- This version disqualifies all former elected officials of the Puerto Rico government from being members of the Board.
- This new version establishes a convoluted way of naming the seven members that will (still) be appointed by the U.S. President:
  - The seven members are divided into six categories identified by letter.
  - The President may select the "member" in Category F in his sole discretion. Once he has selected him or her, the U.S. Congress will submit lists of individuals from which the U.S. President must choose the other six members.
  - Category A "member" should be selected from a list of at least three individuals provided by the Speaker of the House. This member shall maintain a primary residence or have a primary place of business in Puerto Rico.

Would the holder of the controlling share of a multinational corporation doing most of its business in Puerto Rico qualify as having a primary place of business in Puerto Rico?

- Category B "member" should be selected from another list provided by the Speaker of at least three individuals.
- Category C "members" should be selected from a list of at least four individuals provided by the Majority Leader of the Senate.
- Category D "member" should be selected from a list of at least three individuals provided by the Minority Leader of the House.
- Category E "member" should be selected from a list of at least three individuals submitted by the Minority Leader of the Senate.

I suppose there will be two members appointed from Category C since it is the only one that refers to "members" and that is the only way the appointments add to seven.

- The appointments of members in all categories except category F shall be with the advice and consent of the Senate, unless the President appoints an individual from a list.

The bill does not provide for any negotiation between the U.S. President and Members of Congress regarding the lists that the Speaker and the Majority and Minority Leaders will submit. If the President appoints a member from the lists provided, the appointments will not be subject to consent by the Senate.

This provision would come into play only if the President appointed an individual who was not in any of the lists, although this possibility is not expressly contemplated in the bill.

- Members of the Board should be appointed by 30 September 2016. If not, the President shall appoint from the lists generated by the U.S. Congress by 1 December 2016.

This language could be interpreted to permit the President to submit an appointment that is not on a list, even if the nominee would be subject to the advice and consent of the Senate. The soft deadline is 30 September, but the final deadline is two months later.

Two reasons for the delay could be that the President did not have the lists by 30 September, or had them but did not want to appoint any of the individuals included in them. It could be possible that he then has two months to present his own candidates to the consideration of the Senate.

However, that doesn't make much sense, considering the spectacle the U.S. Senate has made with the confirmation process of the nominee to Supreme Court Justice.

- The F3 eliminated the requirement that the Board adopt rules and procedures dealing with conflict of interest.

This could be because they are subject to the Federal conflict of interest requirements, but it still does not look good, particularly since they are expressly authorized to receive gifts.

- The F3 has changed the requirements that the Board has to comply with in order to open additional offices. Now the new offices must be "deemed necessary." The F2 authorized additional offices as the Board "saw fit."

To open additional offices the Board must at least conduct a necessity analysis that justifies the office and, therefore, the expense.

Although, no doubt any office anywhere in the U.S. will always be considered necessary.

- The F3 authorizes the Board to impose the "payment and administration of taxes through the adoption of electronic, reporting, payment and auditing technologies."[1]
- The Board is now authorized to request the Administrator of General Services the support services necessary to carry out its functions.

- The F3 brings major changes to the subpoena powers of the Board. Now, the service of subpoenas and the jurisdiction to compel the attendance of witnesses and the production of documents is subject to Puerto Rico law. This version eliminates the unbridled authorization granted to the Board through which it could have, from anywhere in the U.S., compelled anyone to testify at any place within the U.S. Another change in F3 is that orders related to a subpoena will be issued by Puerto Rico courts and not by the U.S. District Court, as it was in the F2.
- There is a change in the language that protected the autonomy of the Board. This F3 prohibits the Puerto Rico Governor or the Puerto Rico Legislature from enacting or enforcing a law or policy "that would impair or defeat the purposes of this act, as determined by the Oversight Board."[2] The F2 prohibited any like action "with respect to the Oversight Board or its activities."[3]

The change in language could be interpreted as giving more leeway to the Puerto Rico government to control its policy, since now what is prohibited is "impairing or defeating the purposes of" the bill instead of any and every law or policy having to do with the Board.

For example, new legislation dealing with infrastructure security or public document archival would apply to the Board, since it is not something that would "impair or defeat the purposes of" the bill and for those purposes, the Board is an entity of the Puerto Rico government.

Of course, that would be unless the Board determines that the law or policy "impairs or defeats the purposes of" the bill — which I expect will be the Board's typical conclusion.

- The F3 incorporates a reference to the Puerto Rico ethics law applicable to the employees of the Puerto Rico government. It still requires all members and staff of the Board to comply with the Federal conflict of interest requirements "notwithstanding any ethics provision governing employees" of the Puerto Rico government. As to financial disclosure, the F3 is different from the F2 in that the F3 limits the staff required to comply with the disclosure of financial interests to just the staff designated by the Board. F2 imposed that requirement on all the Board's staff.

I do not understand the purpose of these references to Puerto Rico law. It only makes sense if the purpose is to make sure that the staff and Members of the Board comply with the Puerto Rico ethics law.

For employees of the Puerto Rico government this language was not necessary, since they are assigned to the Board on a detail basis and are not considered staff of the Board. Therefore, all Puerto Rico laws applicable to the employees of the Puerto Rico government still apply to every Puerto Rico government employee that is serving in the Board on detail.

- F3 incorporates a requirement that the Board "when feasible" issue a report on the cash flow available for the payment of debt service, as well as any variance from the amount set forth in the debt sustainability analysis.
- This version clarifies that the full faith and credit of the United States is not pledged for the payment of debt issued by Puerto Rico or any of its instrumentalities. The F2 referred to debt issued by the Board.

This draft eliminates the authorization of the Board to issue debt.

## Board Funding

- The F3 eliminates the discretion granted to the Board with respect to its funding, and now it "shall use its powers with respect to the budget" to ensure that enough funds are available to cover all the expenses of the Board.[4] The F2 stated that the Board could use its powers ("may") to appropriate the funds.

Considering the broad powers granted by this bill to the Board, Puerto Rico in practice will end up paying for two government structures — unless it closes down the one we elected and keeps the one "solemnly" imposed by the U.S. Congress.

- The Puerto Rico government is required to designate, within 30 days of the enactment of the bill, a dedicated funding source to maintain the operations of the Board. The F2 had given the Board the discretion of determining whether the BIATS was necessary.

Remember the BIATS discussed in Chapter 1?

## Approval Process of Fiscal Plans and Budgets

- The F3 now requires that all the members be appointed and the Board's Chair be designated before the Board can start the process of approving and certifying fiscal plans and budgets. Under the F2 only four members of the Board had to have been appointed.
- It is now prohibited that resources of a Puerto Rico instrumentality be loaned, transferred, or used for the benefit of Puerto Rico or one of its instrumentalities unless permitted by the Constitution of Puerto Rico.

Yes. Really. F3 has added language to clarify that Puerto Rico cannot violate its Constitution.

- F3 incorporates a new requirement that the Fiscal Plan has to respect the priorities or liens in the Constitution, laws, or agreements of Puerto Rico or its instrumentalities that were in effect prior to the enactment of the bill.

See above.

- In case the Board determines that it will amend a budget because of a variance between real expenses and budgeted expenses, the Board can, in the case of a Puerto Rico instrumentality, prohibit the instrumentality from entering into any contract unless it is previously approved by the Board. In contrast, the F2 specified that the contract had to be in excess of $100,000.

The Board will need enough staff to be a shadow government.

- This version incorporates executive orders issued by the Puerto Rico Governor in the list of documents, contracts, policies, rules, and regulations that the Board can override.
- The F3 prohibits that Puerto Rico enact any law that permits the transfer of funds or assets that is inconsistent with the Constitution or laws of Puerto Rico before the appointment of the seven members of the Board and the designation of its Chair. "Any executive or legislative action autho-

rizing the movement of funds or assets during this time period may be subject to review and reversal by the Board."[5]

This paragraph is absurd. It prohibits Puerto Rico from enacting an unconstitutional law, which, besides being ridiculous, actually is a determination made only by the courts. In addition, the bill states that "any movement of funds or assets" may be subject to review and reversal.

Note that the review and reversal refers to "any movement of funds or assets," while the previous sentence referred to unconstitutional laws. So it appears that the Board, in its sole discretion, infinite knowledge of Puerto Rico law, and special judicial authority, will determine whether a law enacted by the Puerto Rico Legislature is unconstitutional.

Clear separation of the three branches of government?

- The F3 still prohibits the Board from impeding Puerto Rico from implementing laws that execute federal requirements and standards, but only if the laws to be implemented are consistent with a certified Fiscal Plan.

This means that Puerto Rico could be in noncompliance with a federal program if the Board, in its sole discretion, determines that the law necessary to implement the federal program is not consistent with a Fiscal Plan the Board has certified. So, Puerto Rico could end up with the Board appointed by the U.S. government that could impede Puerto Rico's compliance with a federal program.

No doubt about it: overtaking a government is really complicated.

- It is now required that the Fiscal Plan "adopt appropriate recommendations submitted by the Oversight Board."[6] The F2 qualified the adoption of the recommendations "to the greatest extent possible."[7]
- Regarding the areas in which the Board could make recommendations to the Governor or the Legislature, the F3 clarifies that the privatization and commercialization for the delivery of government services really referred to the privatization and commercialization of government entities.

Although the language that stated that the Puerto Rico government could decide not to implement Board recommendations is still in the bill, it is moot. The language added by F3 requires that to be certified a Fiscal Plan must include the recommendations made by the Board.

The "less colonialist" idea did not last long.

## Vieques, That Most Wanted Land

After three versions, each more convoluted than the prior one, F3 gives up and deletes every reference to Vieques.

[12]

# The Czar of the Fire Sales

THIS CHAPTER WILL ANALYZE the changes that the F3 incorporates related to the privatization process of Puerto Rico assets.

## THE CZAR

- In this new version, designating the privatization czar requires the appointment of all seven members of the Board. The F2 required only that four members be appointed.
- F2 required that the Coordinator have substantive knowledge and experience in planning, predevelopment, financing and development of infrastructure projects. F3 adds knowledge and experience in operations, engineering, and market participation of infrastructure projects, but makes them alternative. F2 used "and" and F3 uses "or."

This draft dilutes the qualifications for the privatization czar.

- F3 also adds that stronger consideration will be given to candidates that have experience "with the laws and regulations of Puerto Rico whose implementation could be affected by an Expedited Permitting Process."[1]
- F3 adopts once again the language of F1 and states that the position of the Coordinator will terminate when the Board does. F2 provided that the czar would be in place until all projects had been completed, even if the Board had been terminated.
- However, since the czar's appointment may be terminated before the critical projects are completed, the F3 adds a requirement that the completion of these projects shall continue to be under the expedited permitting process.

## The Process

- F3 incorporates a definition for Project Sponsor which includes, in addition to a private party, a Puerto Rico government agency.
- There are two new requirements for a project submission to be complete. Now a submission also has to include:
  - the amount of Puerto Rico government funds that will be necessary to complete and maintain the project, and

  - the specifics of how many of the jobs created by the project will be held by residents of Puerto Rico and what will be the expected economic impact of the project, including the impact on rate payers.
- F2 required additional information, but only if the project submission referred to an energy project. Although this reference is eliminated and the requirements stayed almost the same, the additional information is not required in its entirety since the "and" of F2 has changed to "or" in F3. The three changes are:
  - Renewable sources of energy will be defined under Puerto Rico law.
  - The goal of achieving "lower energy costs" has changed to "affordable energy rates."

Which are higher than "lower energy costs." Lobbying, lobbying everywhere.

  - Assess how the project will achieve the recommendations of the study that the F3 requires be conducted under the Consolidated and Further Continuing Appropriations Act (the "energy action plan" discussed in Chapter 7) — but only as long as these recommendations are consistent with plans required under Puerto Rico law or with the voluntary agreement negotiated by PREPA with its creditors.

## The Reports

- F3 requires that the critical project report be now developed within 60 days from the project submission. In F2 the 60 days where calculated from the date in which the relevant Puerto Rico agencies where identified.

This change shortens the terms.

- This version clarifies that the Governor must provide a recommendation during the development of the critical project report.
- The F3 now requires that if a project affects the implementation of the Land-Use Plans, the Puerto Rico Planning Board must issue a determination within these 60 days. If the Planning Board determines that the project is not consistent with the Land-Use Plans, the project will be ineligible for a critical project designation.
- F3 eliminates the provision in F2 that if the Puerto Rico Energy Commission did not issue its recommendation within the 60 days, such silence would be deemed a concurrence to the decision taken by the Coordinator. Now, a requirement is added that if a project will connect with PREPA's transmission or distribution facilities, the Energy Commission must determine if the project affects an Approved Integrated Resource Plan. However, differently than in the case of the Land-Use Plans,

the Energy Commission must provide the reason for its determination and the project shall be ineligible for the critical project designation. The determination must be made within the same 60-day time frame.

- The F3 has incorporated a requirement that "immediately following the completion of the critical project report" the report must be made public. The residents of Puerto Rico have a period of 30 days to submit comments. The Coordinator shall respond to them within 30 days and the responses must be made public.
- Under F3, the five days within which the Coordinator must submit its critical project report to the Board start after he or she has responded to the comments provided by Puerto Ricans. Under F2 this submittal to the Board had to be done within five days after the report was finalized.
- Importantly, the F3 eliminated the provision from F2 that if the Board did not decide within 30 days after receiving the critical project report, the project would be deemed a critical project. Now the Board has to affirmatively approve or disapprove the project.

## Stay Out of My Way

- The F3 eliminates the authority that the F2 had granted the Board to disapprove any action the Governor took under Act 76-2000.

See Chapter 5 for a discussion of Act 76-2000.

- F3 keeps the authorization of F2 given to the Board to block the implementation of any law that "may affect the Expedited Permitting Process." However, it has three changes:
  - F2 required that the Governor, the Legislature, and the Coordinator submit to the Board any bill that could affect the expedited process. F3 limits the obligation to the Governor.

I suppose this change was made so the Board receives only one notification instead of three.

  - The F3 requires that the Board review the law to determine if it "adversely impacts" the expedited process. The F2 required that the law "significantly impact" the expedited process.
  - The Board "may" deem such a law to be "significantly inconsistent" with the applicable fiscal plan. Under the F2 the Board had no discretion and "the act shall be deemed to be" significantly inconsistent with the fiscal plan.

This change gives the Board more discretion and limits somewhat the criteria it must consider before deciding to block the application of a law enacted by the Puerto Rico Legislature.

[13]

# The New Restructuring

THIS CHAPTER WILL DISCUSS the changes in F3 related to the restructuring process and to the creditor collective action clauses.

## THE STAY ON LITIGATION

- This new version clarifies that the provisions of the creditor collective action clauses apply to debts created before, on, or after the date of enactment of the bill. The F2 did not expressly apply to the CACs.
- The establishment of the Board does not affect the commencement and the continuation of a proceeding by a governmental unit to enforce its police and regulatory power. Such unit may enforce a judgment other than a money judgment.
- F2 established the end date for the stay as the earlier of (i) 15 February 2017 or (ii) the date when a case was filed under Title III. F3 keeps (ii) as one of the end

dates for the stay, but establishes other possibilities. Now the end date is the earlier of (a) or (b), in which (a) is the date when a case was filed under Title III and (b) is the later of (x) 15 February 2017 or six months after the Board is established; (y) 75 days after the later of the date in (x) if the Board certifies that these additional days are needed to complete the voluntary negotiation process; or (z) 60 days after the date in (x) if the district court so orders after receiving an application under subparagraph 601(l)(1)(D).

This reference does not exist in the bill. The correct reference seems to be 601(m)(1)(D), which refers to the binding effect of the plan of adjustment and the modifications to the debt claims.

This new "formula" tries to take into account that, since all authorization to negotiate and restructure debt has been put in the Board's hands, ending the stay on 15 February 2017 gave it only four months to conduct negotiations on all debt issued by the Puerto Rico government. And that would be if the U.S. President appointed all members by 30 September 2016.

- F3 extends to 45 days the termination of the stay as to a party that had filed with the court a petition for relief. F2 provided that the stay was lifted after 30 days.

- In this version, any person found to have violated the stay is liable for damages, costs, and attorneys fees.
- For purposes of the stay, "Government of Puerto Rico" now includes elected and appointed officials.
- The F3 authorizes the Board in its sole discretion to make interest payments on outstanding debt when such payments become due, even while the stay is in force.
- A new section is added under which Puerto Rico shall be liable to creditors for the value of any property that it transfers if these transfers violate any applicable law that grants the creditor a pledge, security interest, or lien, or that deprives the Puerto Rico instrumentality of property in violation of applicable law. The new section grants a creditor the right to enforce these rights by bringing an action in the U.S. District Court of Puerto Rico, but only after the stay has expired or the creditor has been granted by the court a lift of the stay.

Once again, the bill incorporates a section to prohibit Puerto Rico from violating the law.

## Voluntary Negotiations

- The F3 requires that each creditor or each organized group of creditors that wants to participate in voluntary negotiations with Puerto Rico provide a statement, which will be made public to other participants in the negotiations. The statement must provide:

- the name and address of the creditor
- the name and address of each member of an organized group of creditors
- the nature and the aggregate amount of claims or other economic interests held in relation to the issuer

- An organized group of creditors cannot be composed entirely of affiliates or insiders of one another.

This could be an attempt to incentivize the organization of creditors to facilitate debt negotiations. Prohibiting that a creditors group be composed solely of affiliates is a way of forcing creditors to identify their common claims and negotiate preliminarily amongst them.

- The Board may require that this information be supplemented quarterly.
- The F3 adds requirements for a Puerto Rico issuer to reach a voluntary agreement with creditors:
  - A fiscal plan must be certified as providing for a sustainable level of debt.
    - Or, if the fiscal plan has not been certified, the voluntary agreement must be limited to an extension of principal maturities and interest for a period of up to one year, and during which no interest will be paid.

  - Either the majority in amount of the debt affected by the voluntary agreement vote in favor, or a plan of adjustment has been approved.
- On pre-existing voluntary agreements (which mostly refer to the agreement reached by PREPA and some of its creditors), the F3 now refers to an "executed" agreement instead of a "consummated" agreement as it did in the F2. However, it adds the requirement that the majority in amount of the debt of the issuer agree.

This paragraph has always referred to the PREPA agreement with some of its creditors (who are not the majority in amount as required by this F3).

My comment on Chapter 4 on the change from "successfully reached" to "consummated" applies here, too.

- Holders of a claim can vote on a proposed modification of their claim under Title VI on Voluntary Agreements even if the stay on litigation is in place.

## Restructuring

- The F3 requires that before the Board can issue a certification to authorize a debt restructuring process, it must determine that the entity has made a good-faith effort to reach a restructuring with creditors; that it has put in place the procedures necessary to deliver timely audited financial statements, and "made public draft financial statements and other information sufficient for any interested person to make an informed decision with respect to a possible restructuring;"[1] and that no order has been issued approving a Qualifying Modification, or that, although an order has been issued, the entity cannot make its debt payments.

- The F2 required that the issuer complete the process set forth in Title VI (related to the creditor collective action clauses and voluntary agreements) instead of requiring good-faith efforts in negotiation as in the F3. Also, the F2 required information for an interested person "to perform due diligence." The F3 changed that language "to make an informed decision." The reference to Qualifying Modifications in F3 is new.

- This version adds definitions for "insured bond" and "senior claims."
- F3 states that even if a bond is considered "secured by a lien on property," the issuer, the Board, or any other creditor may challenge the claim or such security, if the modification "is not consummated."
- F3 modifies the definition of "holder of a claim or interest" with respect to who can accept a restructuring plan. The change clarifies that the holder of an insured bond is the monoline insurer.
    - This version excludes the Puerto Rico government and all its instrumentalities from being considered holders of a claim or interest for the purpose of voting on a plan.

- This draft clarifies that the trustee in these restructuring processes is the Board, except as provided in section 926 of the U.S. Bankruptcy Code.
  - This section 926 authorizes the bankruptcy court to appoint a trustee if a debtor refuses to start a cause of action that would avoid fraudulent liens or asset transfers.

Remember that the debtor and the trustee are the same person: The Board. If the Board refused to annul a fraudulent lien or asset transfer, there was not much the court could do since the PROMESA designates the Board as the trustee.

- This version clarifies that, subject to the powers granted to the Board, Puerto Rico is not impaired to exercise its political or governmental powers "whether or not a case has been or can be commenced under this title," except for moratorium laws or "unlawful" executive orders that alter the rights of holders of any debt.

"This title" is Title III that deals with adjustments of debts.

And, once again it will be the Board, instead of the courts, who will, in its sole discretion, determine whether an executive order is unlawful.

- F3 once again incorporates into the bill the possibility that the Board file joint petitions and plans for debtors when they are affiliates. This had been deleted from F2, but it was a provision in F1.

- This version clarifies that the bill does not "permit the discharge of obligations arising under Federal police or regulatory laws."

Although this language is in Title III of the bill, it must be interpreted in conjunction with the language in Title II that opens the possibility that the Board could interfere with the implementation of Puerto Rico laws that are necessary to comply with Federal programs.

- The F3 grants the Board the authorization to consent to a restructuring plan that "interferes" with "any of the political or governmental powers of" Puerto Rico, "any of the property or revenues of" Puerto Rico, and "the use or enjoyment by [Puerto Rico] of any income producing property."[2] F2 stated that it was the debtor, whether Puerto Rico or one of its instrumentalities, who had to consent to this limit to its powers. F3 rips that power from Puerto Rico and grants it to the Board.

So much for "less colonialist."

- This version eliminates the language that provided that the jurisdiction over any person or entity wielded by the district court was "to the fullest extent permitted under the Constitution of the United States."

A cosmetic change, since every court will extend its jurisdiction to the fullest extent permitted by the Constitution.

- The F3 incorporates again the provisions on removal and remand that were in F1 and that F2 had eliminated. Any party can remove any claim to the federal district court in which the civil action is pending.
- A district court has to transfer any civil proceeding that arises under this Title III or is related to a case under this title to the district in which the case is pending.
- This version includes a detailed proceeding of the appeals process.
- This F3 requires that the clerk of the court in which a case of debt restructuring is taking place "reallocate as many staff and assistants as the clerk deems necessary to ensure that the court has adequate resources to provide for proper case management."
- Now the discretion of the Board is broadened: it can "determine in its sole discretion" that the venue is proper in the district court of any jurisdiction in which the Board has an office, other than the one located in Puerto Rico. F2 had required that the Board make a determination that the venue (the District Court of Puerto Rico) could not "adequately provide for proper case management."

- The F3 adds a new section regarding the selection of the U.S. District Court judge who will preside over these cases. If the debtor is Puerto Rico, the judge will be designated by the Chief Justice of the U.S. If the debtor is not a territory, then the presiding judge will be designated by the Chief Judge of the Court of Appeals for the First Circuit.

These three changes must be analyzed together. Under F2, cases under Title III could be litigated outside of Puerto Rico only if the Board determined that the U.S. District Court for Puerto Rico could not adequately manage the case. Now the Board can choose to file these restructuring cases in any other district court in which it has an office.

The U.S. Congress is not worried anymore whether the district court in which the Board files the cases can properly manage them, since it has added the requirement that the clerk of the court chosen by the Board provide all the staff necessary for the cases to be seen in the district court in which the Board wants them to be seen.

New York, New York!

The cases are taken out of the usual process through which cases are assigned to the judges and now are subject to direct assignment. Some experts believe this represents a risk to the U.S. judiciary and that the Chief Justice or the Chief Judge will choose district court judges who have either bankruptcy court experience or some related experience.[3]

I think the "related experience" could also mean experience presiding over sovereign debt litigation.

- F3 adds again the authorization of a district court to abstain from hearing a particular proceeding. This paragraph had been eliminated in F2, although it was in F1.
- This abstention authorization had been included in the F1's section dealing with the certification of issues of Puerto Rico law to the Puerto Rico Supreme Court (discussed in Chapter 4). It had been taken out in F2 and now F3 only adds the authorization to abstain.
- F3 establishes that it is only the Board who may file a plan of adjustment, as well as modifications to the plans already filed. This was the language in F1 — the F2 had substituted debtor for the Board.
- F3 adds a requirement for the confirmation of a plan of adjustment. In F2 the plan had to be feasible and in the best interests of creditors. F3 adds that "shall require the court to consider whether available remedies under the non-bankruptcy laws and [Constitution of Puerto Rico] would result in a greater recovery for the creditors than is provided by such plan."[4]

This language refers to the priority given to the general obligation bonds issued under the full faith and credit of Puerto Rico and that are given first priority in the Constitution of Puerto Rico.

However, adding this language does not weaken the requirement that the plan "be feasible." It is one thing for the creditor to have legal priority and another one for the debtor to have the financial ability to pay.

- This draft authorizes the confirmation of a plan of adjustment when there is a single class of impaired creditors, even if the class did not accept the plan, as long as all requirements of the U.S. bankruptcy code are met.
- F3 adds a section providing for the compensation of professionals employed either by the debtor, the Board, at creditors committee, or a trustee appointed by the court.

## Creditors Get Together

F3 changes the collective action clauses applicable to a restructuring of Puerto Rico debt.

- F3 adds the possibility, just for a preexisting voluntary agreement, that insured and uninsured be classified in different pools and provided different modifications for each, but only if the majority of all uninsured and the majority of all insured bonds agree.

This clarification, most probably added because of the PREPA agreement, is important since the F3 does not consider insurance a factor in how pools will be determined.

- This version requires a minimum voting percentage of bond holders, as well as of the outstanding principal amount. A modification may be made if holders of at least two-thirds of the outstanding amount of principal of each pool vote in favor, and if holders of at least a majority of the bonds outstanding of every pool of the issuer votes in favor.

This is no different than F2 if an issuer has only one pool.

However, if it has more than one pool, every pool must vote for the modification. F3 changed the CAC to a two-tier aggregate majority, since, for a modification to bind every bondholder, it requires a two-thirds majority in amount for the affected pool, and a majority in bonds for the other pools of the issuer.

- F3 specifies that, with respect to these collective action clauses:

> in any judicial proceeding regarding this title, Federal, State, or territorial laws of the United States, as applicable, shall govern and be applied without regard or reference to any law of any international or foreign jurisdiction.[5]

> I presume this section was added because CACs just like the ones added in F3 are mostly seen in bond issues of sovereign debt.

## We Keep Going Back to the Future

The F3 grants immeasurable power to the Board over Puerto Rico's assets and resources. It will be the Board who will decide and who will establish, through the fiscal plans and budgets it "certifies," Puerto Rico's public policy and social priorities.

The F3 did not modify the exemption from liability granted to the Board, its members, and its employees "for any obligation of or claim against the Oversight Board or its members or employees or the territorial government resulting from actions taken to carry out this Act."[6]

This exemption would be sensible if it did not leave the Puerto Rico government as the only party to answer for the claims based on decisions taken, and actions performed, by the Board, its members, and its employees.

The F3 also kept the authorization granted to the Board to conduct business in executive sessions, with only the Board's voting members present and without a requirement to make that information public, intact.

Even the privatization process that is under the absolute control of a Revitalization Coordinator exempts him or her from responsibility. Although the bill states that the Board may take enforcement action related to the privatization program, it refers to a section of the bill that applies only to the Puerto Rico government's employees.

Not only may the Board meet in secret and not disclose the business discussed, but they make decisions and issue orders for which they do not answer, but the people that must follow them do.

I foresee plenty of requests for written, and detailed, instructions.

# [PART 4]

## The Ones Who Can, Vote

[14]

# The Committee

ON 25 MAY 2016 the House Committee on Natural Resources passed the PROMESA bill. The markup of the bill was on 24[1] and 25[2] May, in which the Committee considered 34 amendments, adopted 11, and passed the bill with a vote of 29-10.

## What Is the Voting Process?

Bills are referred to the appropriate committee, which is the one with jurisdiction over the subject matter of the legislation. The committee studies the bill, receives testimonies, and conducts public hearings.

The House Committee on Natural Resources held public hearings on the PROMESA on 12 January 2016, 2 February 2016, 25 February 2016, and 13 April 2016.

> The first and second drafts of the bill were made public after the third hearing (24 and 29 March). The third

draft was introduced in the House the day before the fourth hearing (12 April). The fourth draft, the last, was introduced in the House on 18 May 2016.

After the hearings, the committee decides whether to report a measure; that is, to continue studying the legislation, make needed amendments and, eventually, refer it to the full House for consideration. A bill could also be tabled, which means that no further action will be taken.

The committee meeting in which this is done is called a markup, where amendments are offered, discussed, and voted on. After the markup, the committee usually prepares a report, describing the bill's purposes and provisions, with a recommendation to the Floor to pass the bill and the reasons why. Among the report's contents are an estimate of the bill's cost if it were to become law, and a section-by-section analysis.

The consideration of a bill in the Floor may be governed by a rule, which is a resolution passed by the House that sets out the particulars of the debate for the bill: the amount of time allowed for debate, whether amendments can be offered, etc.

After all debate is concluded and amendments are decided upon, the House votes on the final passage of the bill. Votes may be taken by the electronic voting system which registers each individual member's response. Votes in the House may also be by voice vote, and no record of individual responses is available.

After a measure passes in the House, it goes to the Senate for consideration, where it follows a similar legislative process.

After a measure has been passed in identical form by both the House and Senate, it is considered "enrolled," and it is sent to the President to sign it into law.

## THE AMENDMENTS

The Committee Markup considered 34 amendments. It approved 11, which I will discuss in this Chapter.

### OFFERED BY REPRESENTATIVES GRAVES AND POLIS

This amendment[3] adds a section 410 to the bill, requiring the GAO to submit a report that should describe: the conditions which led to the level of debt per capita and based upon overall economic activity; how actions of the territorial government improved or impaired the territory's financial conditions; and "recommendations on non-fiscal actions, nor policies that would imperil America's homeland and national security, that could be taken by Congress or the Administration to avert future indebtedness of territories, states or local units of government while respecting sovereignty and constitutional parameters."

> The amendment does not establish a due date for this GAO report. Also, the language is confusing. The first paragraph appears to apply to territories, states and their local units of government; the second only to the

territories; and the third to territories, states and their local units of government.

Although the discussion of the amendment centered on an investigation on the causes for the crisis in Puerto Rico, so they can be "lessons learned" applicable to other jurisdictions, the amendment incorporates more inclusive language.

OFFERED BY REPRESENTATIVES GRAVES AND BEYER

Their amendment[4] grants the Board the power to "investigate the disclosure and selling practices in connection with the purchase of bonds issued by" the Puerto Rico government and purchased by retail investors, including "any underrepresentation of risk for such investors and any relationships or conflicts of interest maintained by such broker, dealer, or investment adviser."

Messrs. Graves and Beyer expressed they offered the amendment because they have received complaints about the marketing, disclosures, and sale of Puerto Rico government securities.

Nevertheless, the amendment is very, very interesting, since this is the purview of the Securities and Exchange Commission. It is also an invitation to investigate Wall Street, both the financial firms and the law firms.

Debt issued by Puerto Rico has been transacted with underwriters, brokers, attorneys, and consultants

> from Wall Street firms. I am surprised this was included in the bill.

### OFFERED BY REPRESENTATIVES POLIS AND BENISHEK

This amendment[5] changes the way the Congressional Task Force would be named. Now members must be appointed in coordination with the Chairman of the House Committee on Natural Resources or the Chairman of the Committee on Ways and Means. In the Senate, with the Chairman of the Committee on Energy and Natural Resources or the Chairman of the Committee on Finance. The amendment changes the deadline for the appointment of members to 15 days after enactment, instead of 30. It also adds a requirement that by 15 September 2016 the Task Force must provide a status update to both the House and the Senate.

> The purpose is stated to be to incorporate Committees with jurisdiction on the pro-economic growth measures that the Task Force could recommend. The status update is to give Congress the chance to react to the preliminary findings while it is still in session.

### TWO OFFERED BY REPRESENTATIVE BISHOP OF UTAH

The most important provisions of these[6] amendments[7] are to reincorporate in the bill the provisions of F2 that appointed the Puerto Rico Governor as a member ex officio of the Board, and that established the term of service of the members of the Board, both of which had been eliminated in F3. It also incorporates a change to the language in F2 in the naming of the Chair of the Board, since it now requires that the designation be made within the first 30 days the members of the Board are appointed in full.

It also clarifies that the agreement of a majority in amount of bond claims to a voluntary agreement does not alter the legal rights of holders that did not assent to the agreement.

> It seems to me this amendment kills the possibility of a voluntary agreement under Title VI (the collective action clauses), if dissenting holders can still litigate.
>
> As stated in the discussion, the purpose is to protect PREPA's agreement between PREPA and a number of its bondholders.
>
> This was the only aspect of Mr. Bishop's amendments that was discussed in the markup.

The amendment adds a provision for the reappointment of Members of the Board, and provides for a member of the Board to serve for consecutive terms, as long as the "vacancy on the Oversight Board shall be filled in the same manner in which the original member was appointed."

> Which means, as long as the Member of Congress that provided the list that lead to the nomination of the Member of the Board includes him or her again on the list.

The amendment also eliminates the definition of "senior claim."

### Two Offered by Representative Gallego

One amendment[8] requires that in the case the Congressional Task Force held public hearings, one of them be held in Puerto Rico.

The second amendment,[9] and the only one of the approved amendments that has a roll call (vote 19-18), adds that the Task Force report include a finding regarding Puerto Rico's "equitable access to Federal health care programs."

> A roll call is a vote in which the vote of each Member of Congress is registered and creates a permanent record of the vote.
>
> The main argument against this amendment was presented by Representative Labrador, who said that "what this amendment does it actually puts a stamp on the bill that we [Congress] are asking for additional moneys. We have been attacked as ... people have been saying that this bill is a pathway to a bailout and I think if we actually encourage this task force to look at sending more money to Puerto Rico it will become one and I think that this amendment should be opposed."

### Offered by Representative Hice

This amendment[10] states that the Board may establish policies to require its prior approval to "contracts to a governmental entity or government-owned corporations rather than private enterprise."

> Mr. Hice believes that one of the "key objectives" of the bill should be to "ensure we [Congress] promote and encourage free market competition in order to improve the overall economy of Puerto Rico across all industries," and gives PREPA as one example of what is "way too much reliance on the public sector" and as the reason why the Puerto Rico government has failed.
>
> It seems that for Mr. Hice the provision of intergovernmental services is suspect. Note the language of the amendment: if a governmental entity wants another governmental entity to provide services to it, the Board must approve the contract. Mr. Hice refers only to electric power, but there are also, for example, legal and accounting services that a government entity can offer another.
>
> There must be plenty of U.S.'s corporations with their eyes on the free-market-private-sector-style-every-human-being-is-a-consumer designed by the U.S. Congress for Puerto Rico.

OFFERED BY REPRESENTATIVE MACARTHUR

The amendment[11] adds a section 701 to inform that it is

> the sense of the Congress that any durable solution for Puerto Rico's fiscal and economic crisis should include permanent, pro-growth fiscal reforms that feature, among other elements, a free flow of capital between

> possessions of the United States and the rest of the United States.

This is an example of a "sense of Congress" that expresses an opinion.

Offered by Representative Zinke

His amendment[12] adds a specific study for the Congressional Task Force:

> the economic effect of Administrative Order No. 346 of the Department of Health of the Commonwealth of Puerto Rico (relating to natural products, natural supplements, and dietary supplements) or any successor or substantially similar order, rule, or guidance of the Commonwealth of Puerto Rico.

The Administrative Order[13] to which the amendment refers applies to products sold over-the-counter that label themselves as nutritional supplements, dietary supplements, or "natural" products. The order, that applies provisions of a law enacted in 2004, requires that distributors, and manufacturers, present to the Puerto Rico Department of Health their documentation from the U.S. Food and Drug Administration (FDA) before being able to sell their products in Puerto Rico. This is something that manufacturers should be able to provide their distributors without any problem — if they indeed comply with the FDA.

The Department of Health is trying to improve the safety of the Puerto Rican consumers of these so-called natural products, which is what the Department of Health is supposed to do. And it is doing so by requesting evidence that the distributors and manufacturers of the products comply with the FDA regulations, since the Department of Health has no evidence that they do.

Mr. Zinke argues that this is burdensome because it duplicates what the FDA is doing. He states that the amendment's purpose is to study if this order is affecting U.S. manufacturers who want to grow and manufacture in Puerto Rico, but cannot because of this Administrative Order.

I don't see anything wrong with the Puerto Rico Department of Health requesting evidence of compliance with the FDA regulations on manufacturing and marketing before authorizing the sale of these products over-the-counter in Puerto Rico. But it seems people a lot more powerful than me don't agree.

And interestingly, the Members of Congress that opposed the task force conducting a study on the economic effects of Puerto Rico's limited access to federal health care programs had no objection to voting in favor of this study.

Priorities, priorities.

### Offered by Representative Graves

His other amendment[14] clarifies that "no federal funds shall be authorized by this Act for the payment of any liability of the territory or territorial instrumentality."

> Mr. Graves states that the amendment "is designed to avert a bailout. This provision is designed to make it clear that this legislation does not put federal funds on the table."

## The Voting Roll

The bill was passed in the Committee by a vote of 29-10, with one Representative voting as present. The ten votes against reporting the bill were from Republicans.[15]

[15]

# The Committee Report

THE MARKUP REPORT DESERVES its own chapter. The report prepared by the Committee[1] includes a summary of each section of the bill, and the justification for some of them. It is dated 3 June 2016.

I will include here the language that is most revealing as to the intentions of the U.S. Congress regarding Puerto Rico.

## On the Bill

On the creation of the Board and the appointment of its members, the reports states that the bill:

> provides for the appointment of seven individuals to the Oversight Board through a process that ensures that a majority of its members are effectively chosen by Republican congressional leaders on an expedited timeframe, while upholding the President's constitutional role in making appointments.[2]

As to the lists of nominees, the report clarifies the role of the Senate I discussed in Chapter 11:

> Once the lists are provided, the President has until September 30, 2016, to either select from the lists or appoint someone with the advice and consent of the Senate. If the President fails to appoint the full membership by that deadline, then the President must select candidates from the provided lists before December 1, 2016.[3]

As to preexisting voluntary agreements in section 104(i)(3), the report raises the issue that the protection from scrutiny from the Board granted to these agreements may be used "to justify last-minute, haphazard deals seeking to avoid Oversight Board scrutiny. As such, any clarifications made to this subparagraph will provide a date certain by which voluntary negotiations must have been completed."[4]

The report makes clear that one of the requirements of the fiscal plans is to incorporate all recommendations made by the Board: "these documents incorporate requirements including any recommendation made by the Oversight Board pursuant to Section 205."[5] And the report further states that the "Board may incorporate any recommendations—even those not adopted by the Legislature or Governor—into the development of Fiscal Plans."[6]

> This is the conclusion I reached in Chapter 6. The report leaves no doubt that the Board will be in charge of setting Puerto Rico's public policy and social priorities through its recommendations.

As to the pension obligations, the report states that:

> The Committee acknowledges the concern as to the ambiguity of the language regarding the funding of public pension systems. To clarify, Section 201(b)(1)(C) tasks the Oversight Board with ensuring fiscal plans "provide adequate funding for public pension systems." This language should not be interpreted to reprioritize pension liabilities ahead of the lawful priorities or liens of bondholders as established under the territory's constitution, laws, or other agreements. While this language seeks to provide an adequate level of funding for pension systems, it does not allow for pensions to be unduly favored over other indebtedness in a restructuring.[7]

An attempt to protect all the creditors lobbying for special treatment, and an attempt to try to influence the court presiding over any debt restructuring so that the protections granted to pensioners in municipal bankruptcies in the U.S. not be granted to Puerto Rican pensioners.

As to the court in which the debt restructuring proceedings may be presented, the bill states that it may be the court the Board "determines in its sole discretion." However, the report makes its preference clear: "In the case of Puerto Rico, venue will probably be in the District of Columbia."[8]

It seems I've been singing to the wrong city.

The report emphatically asserts that the privatization of Puerto Rico assets — the "infrastructure revitalization" — is "premised" on Puerto Rico's Act 76-2000.[9]

> Chapter 5 discusses the provisions of Act 76-2000 and how its purpose is cynically perverted by the U.S. Congress in this bill.

As to the eligibility of critical infrastructure projects, the report clarifies that:

> The Committee does not intend for projects that are not approved to be Critical Projects or that are deemed to be ineligible for Critical Project designation to be precluded from reapplying for Critical Project designation. If a project receives an adverse ruling, the Committee would encourage the project proponent to amend his or her proposal, and resubmit it for Critical Project designation.[10]

> So in this report the House Committee on Natural Resources is "encouraging" proponents that fail to prove their projects are "critical" to try again. The bill sets a process that the privatization czar and the Board must follow, but the Members of the Committee apparently feel the need to cheer the proponents from afar. Goodness.

The report incorporates the cost estimate prepared by the Congressional Budget Office, which I discuss in the next chapter.

### Additional Views

The report also incorporates additional views by Representative Pierluisi (Puerto Rico's sole representative in the U.S. Congress, with no right to vote), and Representative Grijalva.

> "Additional views" means that they are not consensus views of the Committee, but that reflect only the views of their authors.

## Puerto Rico's Representative

The following views by Mr. Pierluisi are worth noting:

> H.R. 5278 is exceptional insofar as it was negotiated in a painstakingly bipartisan manner at an intensely partisan time in American political life, and inasmuch as it has been successful to date despite a well-funded and often dishonest lobbying campaign against the bill. The bill is imperfect—as all compromises by definition are—but it is also indispensable for my constituents. Of this I have no doubt. At the May 25, 2016 markup of H.R. 5278, a bipartisan coalition of Committee members remained united to defeat multiple amendments designed to kill or severely weaken the bill. Amendments that were adopted strengthen the bill or are purely technical in nature.
>
> Many commentators, including some of my congressional colleagues, like to cite one cause of the crisis in Puerto Rico, namely mismanagement at the local level. But they ignore the other cause of the crisis, which is inequality at the federal level enabled by Puerto Rico's

> status as a territory—rather than a state—of the United States. It may give such commentators comfort to blame everything on Puerto Rico, but it is a false comfort rooted in a flawed reading of history. The second-class treatment my constituents are subjected to, a consequence of our second-class status, must end. It will not happen in PROMESA, but I am confident it will happen soon.[11]

The ten votes in the Committee against reporting the bill were by Republicans. According to news reports, the main reason given by those that spoke publicly was that Puerto Rico should not have any possibility of restructuring its debt.

The eighteenth- and nineteenth-century debtor's prison is alive and well.

> The Puerto Rico government and the oversight board should work together as partners for prosperity, not as petty rivals for power. If the Puerto Rico government does its job well, the board will have a limited role and will cease to operate within a few years.[12]

In this, I disagree. Such a behavior from the U.S. and its representatives would require an almost 180-degree change in its historical attitude towards Puerto Rico.

I am not as hopeful as our Representative seems to be. But, yes, I would love to be proved wrong.

As to the lowering of the minimum wage for young workers, Mr. Pierluisi states:

> In an otherwise bipartisan bill, this is the only instance where ideology can be said to have trumped intelligence. Nevertheless, I do not anticipate that the Puerto Rico government will ever use this authority, so its practical impact will be zero. Therefore, it is not worth discarding the broader bill over this misguided, but ultimately meaningless, provision.
>
> The most likely result of exempting Puerto Rico from the federal minimum wage would be to discourage individuals from working in the formal economy, to encourage more individuals to work in the informal economy, to provide an additional incentive for individuals to rely upon government assistance programs rather than to work, and to increase the already-historic level of migration from Puerto Rico to the states. I am not aware of a single economist in Puerto Rico who has argued otherwise.[13]

As to the powers and responsibilities of the Board, Mr. Pierluisi believes that:

> In general, the oversight board, which is not a federal entity, will provide guardrails for the Puerto Rico government, but will not supplant or replace the territory's elected leaders, who will retain primary control over budgeting and fiscal policymaking.
>
> The goal is for the governor and the board to work together for the benefit of the people of Puerto Rico, not to have parallel governing structures.[14]

Unsurprisingly, I believe these statements are misleading. If all decisions, laws, regulations, and budgets are subject to the Board's approval, the Puerto Rico government does not have "primary control over budgeting and fiscal policymaking." In addition, the over-broad authority of review and approval granted to the Board requires a parallel governing structure if the Board is to comply with the responsibilities granted to it by this bill.

It is one thing to speculate on how the Board would behave and how willing it would be to work as advisor to the Puerto Rico government instead of its supervisor. But I base my admittedly pessimistic analysis on what the bill explicitly grants the Board, and on how the U.S. appointees have historically behaved towards Puerto Rico, as well as on the statements made by Members of the U.S. Congress who will be submitting candidates to the Board.

Under the bill, the Puerto Rico government and its elected representatives have been demoted to clerks for the Board. Just because the Puerto Rico government may prepare the first drafts of budgets and plans does not mean it has "primary control over budgeting and fiscal policymaking."

The "multiple opportunities" "granted" to the Puerto Rico government to answer the Board's objections, which are being touted by Mr. Pierluisi and other Members of Congress as proof of the Puerto Rico government's control, are just "multiple opportunities" to comply with instructions.

Finally, as to Puerto Rico's political status and its effect on economic growth:

> The American public and their elected representatives must come to terms with a fundamental fact, which is that the main cause of Puerto Rico's economic, fiscal and demographic problems is its undemocratic and unequal political status.
>
> Puerto Rico's status as a territory is not an abstract or theoretical problem. It is a moral, social and political wrong with crushing practical consequences for the men, women and children I represent.
>
> The time has come for my constituents to have equality in this union or to have independence outside of it.[15]

None as blind as those who refuse to see.

[16]

# The Still Unknown Cost of Control

ON 25 MAY 2016 the House Committee on Natural Resources ordered the Congressional Budget Office to prepare a cost estimate for the implementation of the PROMESA.

The CBO issued its report[1] on 3 June 2016 and issued an estimated cost of $370 million for the Board's operations.

The report concludes that the "control board"[2] established under the bill is a "federal entity" because of "the significant degree of federal control" involved in its establishment and operations. Therefore, the cash flows related to the Board's administrative costs should be recorded in the federal budget.

## The Reimbursements

The CBO calculates that for the period 2017-2026 the costs of operating the Board would be $370 million. However, since the costs would be paid by the Puerto Rico government and transferred to the U.S. government, the "control board" would "have no significant net effect on the federal deficit." Although the bill specifies that the "control board" shall not be considered part of the U.S. government, the CBO states that since the activities of the Board are federal activities, they should be included in the federal budget.

The amounts provided by Puerto Rico to fund the Board's operations should be recorded in the federal budget as revenue, and the expenditures should be recorded as federal direct spending.

## The Costs of the Board

The CBO estimates in $1 million the 2017 costs of preparing the several reports required by the bill, as well as the expenses of its administrative requirements.

These are the CBO's estimates of the Board's expenditures in the years 2017-2022:

| | |
|---|---|
| 2017 | $200 million |
| 2018 | $150 million |
| 2019 | $5 million |
| 2020 | $5 million |
| 2021 | $5 million |
| 2022 | $5 million |

The period 2017-2022 totals $370 million, and the cost estimated by the CBO for 2023-2026 is zero.

In addition to the $1 million in 2017 that the CBO estimates is needed for the preparation of reports and the payment of administrative costs, it estimates that the discretionary costs of implementing the bill would increase by less than $500 thousand in subsequent years.

> Which I understand to mean only from 2018–2022, since that is the period the CBO considers the Board will be active.

In its analysis, the CBO

> examined the administrative costs — particularly for legal and financial expertise required to oversee procedures related to bankruptcy and debt restructuring — incurred by institutions involved in resolving financial crisis faced by U.S. municipalities, including Detroit, Philadelphia, New York City, and the District of Columbia.[3]

Quoting a Bloomberg report from 2015, the CBO states that Puerto Rico and PREPA have spent over $60 million in legal and financial advisory services. It also reports that officials of the Puerto Rico government indicated to the CBO that they anticipated spending around $75 million in 2017 for these purposes.

The CBO also received information from the U.S. Department of the Treasury "about the likely costs to operate the Puerto Rican oversight board." The CBO

> expects that the board would spend roughly twice as much as the city of Detroit over the next two years to restructure [its] debt and to prepare balanced budgets.[4]

The CBO expects that of the total estimate of $370 million for six years, $350 million would be spent "within the first two years and would primarily cover fees of legal and financial consultants hired to restructure Puerto Rico's debt."[5] The CBO estimates that once the restructuring is achieved, the Board would spend just $5 million yearly

> to help the Puerto Rico government prepare and execute balanced budgets for the next four consecutive years as required by the bill — or through fiscal year 2022.[6]

The CBO prepared its estimate assuming that the Board's expenses would be transferred directly to the Board by the Puerto Rico government as needed to pay expenses, although they would be recorded in the Federal government's budget.

## The Puerto Rico Costs

Considering the all-encompassing powers and discretion that the bill gives the Board, the CBO estimates that

> [Puerto Rico] public entities would spend several hundred million dollars over the next several years to

> comply with the board's requirements and to implement new fiscal plans. CBO expects that most of those costs would be incurred in the first few years after enactment of the legislation, when the board would be active.[7]

## THE TWO MAIN ISSUES WITH THIS ESTIMATE

As to the operating costs of the Board, the CBO based its estimate on the costs of the debt restructuring incurred by the city of Detroit, which had outstanding debt of $18 billion. The CBO states it doubles the amount, distributes it over the first two years the Board will be in operations, and calls it a day.

1. Detroit is a city with, obviously, a government structure simpler than Puerto Rico's.
2. Detroit's debt restructuring was conducted within a bankruptcy proceeding, which is not the process that may be used to restructure Puerto Rico debt.
3. Restructuring a city's debt of $18 billion is quite different than restructuring a country's debt of $70 billion issued by 18 different but related entities and that may have overlapping sources of payment.
4. The CBO's estimate does not reflect the methodology the CBO states it used. The CBO report states that "the city of Detroit spent more than $170 million over a period of about 18 months for the services of legal and financial firms to manage bankruptcy proceedings related to that city's $18 billion in public debt."[8] The projection of that amount over two years is

$226 million, which doubled, as the CBO says it did, would be over $450 million. Why is the CBO's estimate for these two years for this purpose $350 million?

5. The CBO's estimate of $350 million is only based on the costs of "services of legal and financial firms to manage bankruptcy proceedings" and is the total cost estimated by the CBO for the operation of the Board.
6. The CBO did not estimate the cost of operating the Board, nor the costs of its staff and reimbursement of the Board Members' expenses, for those first two years. It estimated only the cost of debt restructuring. The estimate does not include any costs for all the other tasks the Board has been assigned in the bill.
7. The CBO ignores the costs of the Revitalization Coordinator, as well as the costs of advisors the Board may want to have for other issues unrelated to debt restructuring.
8. For years 2019-2022, the CBO estimates the cost of operating the Board in only $5 million per year, but does not explain the methodology it used to reach this estimate. Does this include the cost of all staff, advisors, and legal and financial consultants?

The $370 million for 2017-2022 is a low-ball number not justified even by the analysis that the CBO says it conducted, and ignores all the other tasks the Board has been assigned in this bill; tasks that go beyond anything that the overseers of the debt restructuring in Detroit had to do.

The yearly estimate of $5 million is also very low, considering all the staff the Board will need to comply with everything this bill requires it to do.

The second issue is the costs in which the Puerto Rico government will have to incur to comply with the requests the Board makes, as well as "those stemming from decisions made by the control board established under the bill."[9] The CBO mentions that these costs are estimated "in the several hundred million dollars"[10] for the years the "board would be active," which the CBO estimates is until 2022. How much is "several"? Three hundred million? Four hundred million? Nine hundred million? The CBO report doesn't say.

Although, in all fairness, it doesn't have to. The CBO concerns itself with the federal budget and federal costs, and not the costs that a bill from the U.S. Congress would generate for the Puerto Rico government.

However, the report raises the point, even if broadly, that the bill would increase the costs to Puerto Rico by "several hundred million dollars," even if it does not discuss the impact these considerable costs will have in the implementation of the bill, a possible restructuring of the debt, and Puerto Rico's fiscal health.

## The Final Number

The only cost estimate that I could extract from this report is that the expenses exclusively related to legal and financial expertise for debt restructuring may be $450 million for the first two years (if I follow the methodology described in the report.)

There is no estimate for the total cost of the Board, since it is not clear if "the services of legal and financial firms" includes the cost of the Board's staff and the costs of other consultants whose services are not related to debt restructuring.

> If indeed it does not include any of these factors, the CBO's estimate of $400 million for the first two years of the Board's operation is so low it is unusable.

[17]

# The House

THE PROMESA BILL WAS voted by the U.S. House of Representatives on 9 June 2016. The House agreed to seven amendments, and passed the bill with a vote of 297-127.

## Rules for Discussion and Debate

When a bill is reported out[1] of a House Committee, it is usually considered by the Committee on Rules to determine the rules under which the bill will be debated in the Floor and how amendments to the bill will be offered.

In the case of this bill, the Committee on Rules determined[2] that only eight amendments would be considered, out of 39 submitted.[3]

## The Court Lights Their Way

In a masterful stroke of timing in support of the U.S. Congress, on the morning the bill would be considered by the House of Representatives, the U.S. Supreme Court issued an opinion on one of two cases it had before its consideration that raised issues on Puerto Rico's self-government and autonomy.

Unsurprisingly, in a 6-2 opinion delivered by Justice Kagan, former U.S. Solicitor General nominated to the Court by President Obama, the Court held[4] that Puerto Rico lacks sovereignty; that what little self-government it may have flows from what the U.S. Congress may deign to grant it; and that it is still today subject to the plenary powers of the U.S. Congress.

The Court applied a "historical test"[5] based on the Insular Cases, and never disapproved their racially-charged and bigoted language and "legal" justification.

The Court, with impeccable timing, put paid to the arguments that the PROMESA violated Puerto Rico's self-government as well as the representations the U.S. government gave the United Nations about the extent of Puerto Rico's self-government and the nature of its new relationship to the U.S.

> By holding that the source of Puerto Rico's self-government is the U.S. Congress, it confirms, once again, that the door is wide-open for the U.S. Congress to approve whatever kind of government, rule, or control it may want to impose upon Puerto Rico, whenever it seems fit and under whatever conditions it seems fit.
>
> That's plenary power, from Congress and from the Court.

For those who have read about this, the opinion came as no surprise, even if the Court, undoubtedly, could have been more elegant and less obvious in its timing.

Therefore, in 2016 it bases what it calls a "historical test" on racist opinions of 1901; still sees itself as protector of the imperialistic aspirations of the U.S.; and blithely ignores the representations the U.S. gave to the United Nations regarding Puerto Rico's colonial condition.

The Court refers to the "chain" that binds Puerto Rico to the U.S. Congress,[6] and I've talked about the shackles: these are the U.S. exceptionalism and plenary power that gives us the Foraker 21.

## THE AMENDMENTS

Of the eight amendments debated, seven were agreed to.

### OFFERED BY REPRESENTATIVE BISHOP OF UTAH

The most important changes of his amendment[7] as to Puerto Rico are to set 1 September 2016 as the date the members of the Board must be appointed (from 30 September), and 15 September as the final deadline (from 1 December).

It also specifies that the voluntary agreements between Puerto Rico government issuers and creditors must have been reached before 18 May 2016 (the date the final draft of the bill was introduced in the House). It also extends to one year the due date of the GAO report on Puerto Rico's

HUBZones (from 180 days), and eliminates states and local units of government from the report required from the GAO on the territories' level of debt and financial condition.

The amendment also authorizes the presence of "professionals the Oversight Board determines necessary" during the executive sessions carried out by the Board.

It also clarifies that, in the matter of voluntary agreements, the legal rights of bondholders that had not consented to the voluntary agreement are not altered, but only until a court order approves the terms of the agreement.

This takes care of the problem I raised in Chapter 14.

Another provision of the amendment provides for the initial funding of the Board. It requires that as soon as the Board is established, and on the fifth day of each month, the Puerto Rico government transfer to the Board for its use the amount determined by the Board, which will not be less than $2 million monthly. If eventually the Board decides the amounts it has requested and received exceeds what it requires for its operations, the Board shall "periodically" remit the moneys to the Puerto Rico government. This monthly transfer will terminate as soon as the BIATS is designated.

Remember the BIATS? I discussed it in Chapter 1.

The amendment also grants the Board the power to rescind any law enacted between 4 May 2016 and the appointment of all members of the Board, as long as the law "alters pre-existing priorities of creditors in a manner outside the ordinary course of business or inconsistent with [Puerto Rico's] constitution or [its] laws."

> This refers to a law enacted on 5 May 2016 related to the powers of the Government Development Bank for Puerto Rico's receiver, and the priority in which the bank's liabilities would be paid if a receiver was appointed.[8]

Mr. Bishop's amendment incorporates two factors the Board "may consider" when determining in which court a debt restructuring proceeding may be filed: "the resources of the district court," and "the impact on witnesses."

> This is a cosmetic amendment, since the Board "may consider" these factors, but does not have to. It is still empowered to determine "in its sole discretion" in which court the restructuring proceedings will be filed. This requirement looks nice on paper, but does not limit in any way the Board's discretion.

As to the Revitalization Coordinator, the amendment eliminates the prohibition that the candidate could not have provided "goods or services to the government of Puerto Rico" "in the preceding 3 calendar years."

> This broadens the pool of candidates.

As to the other territories, the amendment eliminates the paragraph that provided that a Board could be established for a territory under the PROMESA if the legislature adopted a resolution requesting it. To mitigate any issue of unconstitutionality because of different treatment to territories (Puerto Rico versus the others), the amendment adds a paragraph providing that if a territory requested that a Board be imposed upon it, the bill would be extended to it.

> If only the bill had been drafted like this from the very beginning! Then it would not have all these sentences with interminable references to "territories" and "territorial" and clumsy attempts to make it apply to everyone.
>
> The bill would have been much cleaner, instead of this reported bill that makes for such awkward reading.

OFFERED BY REPRESENTATIVE GRAVES

The amendment[9] clarifies that the Board cannot take actions that "impede" the Puerto Rico government to "preserve and maintain federally funded mass transportation assets."

> The purpose of the amendment is to make the maintenance of mass transportation assets a priority for the Board, since part of the cost was funded with a contribution from the U.S. government.

### Offered by Representative Jolly

The amendment[10] requires that the report issued by the U.S. Congress Task Force on Puerto Rico's economic growth include recommended changes to federal law and programs that would serve to reduce child poverty.

### Two Offered by Representative Byrne

The first[11] of the two amendments offered by Representative Byrne establishes 18 months as the due date for the report the GAO must prepare on the territories' level of debt and financial condition.

The other amendment[12] requires the GAO to prepare another report. It will have to be submitted to Congress within a year after the PROMESA is enacted, and then at least every two years. The report, on the public debt of each territory, must include current levels and projections of both revenue and debt; identify the drivers of debt; the ability of the territory to repay its debt; as well as "the effect of Federal law, mandates, rules, and regulations on each territory's public debt."

### Offered by Representatives Duffy and Pierluisi

The amendment[13] would eliminate a census cap (based on population) that applies when determining eligibility for the HUBZone program.

> The purpose of the amendment is to mitigate, for ten years or while the Board is active, the cap that disproportionally disqualifies Puerto Rico's small

> businesses from the program, since the number of communities in Puerto Rico that qualify as "distressed" under the HUBZone program exceed the census cap.

### Offered by Representatives Serrano and Velázquez

The amendment[14] clarifies that the Puerto Rico Commission for the Comprehensive Audit of the Public Credit may keep conducting its investigations and filing its reports, and for the Puerto Rico government or the Board to review and consider its findings.

> The Commission was created by Puerto Rico Act 97-2015 to audit the debt of government issuers.[15]

## The Voting Roll

The House passed the bill with a vote of 297-127. 158 Democrats voted in favor; 24, against. Of the Republican Representatives, 139 voted in favor; 103, against. Five Republicans and six Democrats did not vote.[16]

## The Record of the Discussions

The debates[17] on both the resolution establishing the rules for the debate and voting of the PROMESA, as well as the debate of the bill, are available in the Congressional Record for 9 June 2016.

[18]

# The Senate

THE SENATE PASSED THE PROMESA on 29 June 2016 with a final vote of 68-30.

## The Pressure's On

The bill passed in the House and was received in the U.S. Senate on 13 June 2016. The discussions about it started with the backdrop of a default by Puerto Rico government issuers on 1 July for total payments of almost $2 billion.

Many Senators opposed the bill: some called it colonialist, others wanted to require the participation of Puerto Ricans as members of the Board, and others wanted the opportunity to offer amendments.

Meanwhile, the U.S. Treasury was stepping up the pressure for the Senate to approve the bill before 1 July, so that the stay on litigation would be in place when the default happened.

The Senate leaders were also under pressure because the House of Representatives was in recess until 5 July. That meant that if the bill was amended in the Senate, the amendments could not be considered by the House until after the default.

And since the U.S. Supreme Court had held that only the U.S. Congress, under the territorial clause of the U.S. Constitution, had the power to act on the issue (since the Court decided Puerto Rico did not have any), there was nowhere the Senate could turn for a reprieve, if it indeed wanted to have the stay on litigation in place by 1 July.

The bill was brought to a vote in the Senate on 29 June, after limiting the time for debate and the offer of amendments. It was presented to the President on 30 June 2016, who that day signed it into Public Law 114-187.[1]

## SCOTUS, Once More

Coincidentally, on 13 June, the day the bill was received in the Senate, the U.S. Supreme Court issued the second opinion on Puerto Rico's self-government on the other case that it had under its consideration. Again unsurprisingly, this time in an opinion delivered by Justice Thomas, the Court held[2] that the U.S. Congress could exclude Puerto Rico from authorizing its municipalities from filing bankruptcy under Chapter 9, and was also barred from authorizing its own law.

> In a reading that must have every single one of the 50 states trembling for their sovereignty under the

> Tenth Amendment (see Chapter 8) of the U.S. Constitution (and considering that their sovereignty was not the subject of the case), the Court held that Puerto Rico was as barred from authorizing its bankruptcy law for its municipalities, just as every one of the 50 states was barred from authorizing its own law outside of Chapter 9, even if the state had decided not to authorize its municipalities to use it.[3]

As to the reasons why Puerto Rico's law was enacted, precisely the lack of a debt restructuring process, the Court said that it could not "rewrite" the law the U.S. Congress had written.

> The Court determined that the case was an issue of legal interpretation, and therefore ignored its own precedents that required that the U.S. Congress justify discriminatory treatment for Puerto Rico.
>
> And in an attempt to ignore the related issues of Puerto Rico's self-government and political status, the Court used an argument that hobbles the sovereignty of the 50 states under the Tenth Amendment of the U.S. Constitution.
>
> So, in short, the Court said: "The hot potato is all yours, Congress. Territory. Plenary power. Do as you see fit."

## The Voting Roll

The Senate passed the bill with a vote of 68-30. Thirty-one (31) Democrats voted in favor; 11, against. Of the Republican

Senators, 36 voted in favor; 18, against. Of the independents, one voted in favor; one, against. Two Democrats did not vote.[4]

## The Record of the Discussions

The debates on both the cloture vote establishing the limits for the debate and the offer of amendments, as well as the debate on the bill, are available in the Congressional Record for 27 June[5] and 29 June[6] 2016.

# [PART 5]

## The Ones Who Can't Vote, Speak

# [19]

# Conclusion

THE ANALYSIS PREPARED BY the Congressional Research Service dated 1 July 2016 is a good reference to the PROMESA.[1] It includes a section-by-section summary and analysis of the bill, as well as a list of other legislative measures presented in the U.S. Congress to address Puerto Rico's fiscal situation.

The PROMESA, even if taken as an attempt full of good faith and better intentions, falls short of confronting the fundamental reasons for Puerto Rico's debt crisis: lack of economic growth; lack of medium- and long-term planning; and the lack of political tools to establish them.

Someone else is making (and changing) the rules under which Puerto Rico has to operate. Lack of control over legislation, rules, and regulations take a toll on social and economic planning. Being subject to international treaties that protect other jurisdictions and sacrifice Puerto Rico makes it impossible to draft comprehensive long-term economic development strategies.

The law wants to provide a solution for creditors in the midst of an economic depression that doesn't provide enough cash for full payment. But budget cutting and austerity will not provide creditors with the astronomical returns they want.

## The Congressional Task Force

### Members

The eight members of the Task Force are the Republicans Orrin Hatch (who is its Chair) and Marco Rubio from the Senate, and Sean Duffy and Tom MacArthur from the House. The four Democrats are Bill Nelson and Robert Menéndez from the Senate, and Nydia Velázquez and Pedro Pierluisi from the House.

### Committees

I thought it would be interesting to see to what congressional committees the members of the Task Force are assigned. And this is what I found:

1. Senator Hatch is a member of the Committees on Finance; the Judiciary; and Health, Education, Labor and Pensions.
2. Senator Rubio is a member of the Committees on Foreign Relations; Commerce, Science and Transportation; Small Business and Entrepreneurship; as well as of the Select Committee on Intelligence.

3. Senator Nelson is a member of the Committees on Armed Services; Finance; Commerce, Science and Transportation; as well as of the Special Committee on Aging.
4. Senator Menéndez is a member of the Committees on Foreign Relations; Finance; and Banking.
5. Representative Duffy is a member of the Committee on Financial Services.
6. Representative MacArthur is a member of the Committees on Armed Services; and Natural Resources.
7. Representative Velázquez is a member of the Committees on Financial Services; and Small Business.
8. Representative Pierluisi is a member of the Committees on the Judiciary; and Natural Resources.

I expected that members of the Task Force would belong to committees on finance, banking, or small business.

But I wanted to know how many were assigned to committees related to foreign affairs or armed forces. The answer? Half of the Task Force.

My question was based on the geopolitical importance that Puerto Rico[2] has for the U.S.; the increase of the U.S.'s military presence in Puerto Rico in the last year; and the argument that Puerto Rico cannot be exempted from the cabotage law (the Merchant Marine Act of 1920) because of U.S. national security.

## Coincidence?

It is intriguing that both Senators from Florida are part of the Task Force.

It could be because of the high number of immigrants from Puerto Rico that Florida has been receiving during the last few years.

But it cannot be overlooked that the main companies that ship to Puerto Rico under the Merchant Marine Act of 1920, and the highest number of jobs generated by that cabotage law, are in Florida. And that Puerto Rico has been requesting for years now to be exempted from the law.

Neither can it be overlooked that both Senators belong to the Senate Committee with primary jurisdiction over the merchant marine.

Since Puerto Rico generates 25% of the revenues[3] of the merchant marine companies (and Puerto Rico's population is equivalent to about 1% of the U.S. population), that should give you an idea of the importance of analyzing why both Senators from Florida could have been named to the Task Force.

I find it probable that the Task Force would follow the same reasoning that the PROMESA requires of the GAO's report and that it would restrict its recommendations to those "on non-fiscal actions, or policies that would not imperil America's homeland and national security."[4]

Armed forces, intelligence, foreign relations, merchant marine. Too much coincidence sometimes is no coincidence at all.

## VOTERS BEWARE

As to the PROMESA, I think it will be very difficult to implement and that it will cost considerably more than the estimates provide.

The law gives the Board so much power that it has given its members no scapegoat. They will be the only ones responsible for the results that the Board accomplishes (or not). They will be the ones ultimately responsible for the cuts to public services, since its members are the ones who certify budgets and fiscal plans.

### ECONOMIC GROWTH

These budgets and fiscal plans are based exclusively on expenditure control, because no real discussion was ever had in the U.S. Congress about the many constraints the U.S. imposes upon Puerto Rico's economic development in the medium- and long-term.

It wasn't until the fourth draft of the bill (F3) that a task force was created to study the "impediments in current Federal law and programs to economic growth in Puerto Rico."[5] But as I discussed, that would entail an honest look at the plenary power the U.S. Congress exercises over Puerto Rico, which I very much doubt they are willing to do.

And that is a risk for the Board. The PROMESA is based on an ideology that predicates plenty of austerity for Puerto Ricans. What will happen when the Board cannot get results because the economy, even with the Board in charge, keeps spiraling down? There will be no Puerto Rican politician to blame.

## THE COSTS

Complying with all the duties and responsibilities that the law imposes upon the Board will require a large staff. Even if most work is done through consultants, it will require a considerable administrative structure.

The PROMESA requires deep knowledge of the Puerto Rico government structure, of governmental priorities of social and public services, as well as of regulations and procedures, because even if it wanted to, the Board cannot start from scratch.

Reviewing budgets, preparing fiscal plans, supervising the accounting and the collections of revenues and the payments of expenditures, and all the other micromanagement tasks that the PROMESA imposes on the Board, requires much more than a skeleton crew.

The cost estimates published by the CBO are woefully low. And no usable estimate has been done on the several hundreds of millions of dollars that the Puerto Rico government will have to incur to comply with the requirements of the Board.

The PROMESA increases considerably the costs for the Puerto Rico government, while making a point of imposing austerity. It will be difficult for the Board to make this work.

## Collaboration

Implementing the law also requires cooperation from the employees of the Puerto Rico government, who are, by the PROMESA's provisions, responsible for all claims brought because of the decisions and actions taken by the Board and its staff.

The Board will be received with a lot of mistrust. It was conceived as a supra-structure to get creditors paid, sell our assets, and leave Puerto Rico to pick up the results (and the claims) of the Board's decisions. It will take a long time to establish a trustful and workable relationship with the Puerto Rico government's employees, who are the fundamental participants for the Board to be able to even start its job.

These employees are the ones who know how the government works, how instrumentalities share information, have the historical knowledge and can explain why things are done the way they are, and what works and what doesn't, what was considered before and why it was discarded. The Board needs to woo these employees, so they see the Board and its staff as allies. If not, there are plenty of pitfalls in which the Board will fall.

## Expectations

When the U.S. government was trying to convince Puerto Ricans that the Board was the best solution and that the takeover of the Puerto Rico government by this group of seven private persons was justified, the U.S. government created unrealistic expectations of what the Board would accomplish.

Since it repeated the argument that the crisis was the sole responsibility of Puerto Rico's politicians, and excluded all other factors, many people in Puerto Rico expect miracles from the Board — since, after all, they are not the Puerto Rican politicians who were the sole cause of the crisis.

Unmet unrealistic expectations are the worst, and the Board will have many to face.

In the end, the PROMESA embodies the obliviousness of the metropolis. The law's acronym reflects the promise of control exercised over the colony — as blessed by the metropolis's judicial system.

Foraker 21.

[20]

# Back to the Future in 1898

PROCLAMATION OF NELSON A. MILES, Commanding General of the U.S. Army in charge of the invasion of Puerto Rico, on 28 July 1898:

> To the Inhabitants of Porto Rico [sic]:
>
> In the prosecution of the war against the kingdom of Spain by the people of the United States, in the cause of liberty, justice, and humanity, its military forces have come to occupy the island of Porto Rico [sic]. They come bearing the banner of freedom, inspired by a noble purpose to seek the enemies of our country and yours, and to destroy or capture all who are in armed resistance. They bring you the fostering arm of a free people, whose greatest power is in its justice and humanity to all those living within its fold. Hence the first effect of this occupation will be the immediate release from your former relations, and it is hoped a cheerful acceptance of the government of the United States. The chief object of the American military forces will be to overthrow the armed authority of Spain, and to

> give the people of your beautiful island the largest measure of liberty consistent with this occupation. We have not come to make war upon the people of a country that for centuries has been oppressed, but, on the contrary, to bring you protection, not only to yourselves, but to your property; to promote your prosperity, and bestow upon you the immunities and blessings of the liberal institutions of our government. It is not our purpose to interfere with any existing laws and customs that are wholesome and beneficial to your people so long as they conform to the rules of military administration of order and justice. This is not a war of devastation, but one to give all within the control of its military and naval forces the advantages and blessings of enlightened civilization.

Could have been written today.

[21]

# Suggested Readings

## Books

- Nelson A. Denis, *War Against All Puerto Ricans: Revolution and Terror in America's Colony* (New York: Public Affairs Books, 2015).
- Gerald L. Neuman and Tomiko Brown-Nagin, eds., *Reconsidering the Insular Cases: The Past and Future of the American Empire* (Cambridge: Harvard University Press, 2015).
- Juan R. Torruella, *Global Intrigues: The Era of the Spanish-American War and the Rise of the United States to World Power* (San Juan: Editorial de la Universidad de Puerto Rico, 2008).
- Jorge Rodríguez Beruff, *Strategy As Politics: Puerto Rico on the Eve of the Second World War* (San Juan: Editorial de la Universidad de Puerto Rico, 2007).

- Bartholomew H. Sparrow, *The Insular Cases and the Emergence of American Empire* (Lawrence: University Press of Kansas, 2006).
- Christina Duffy Burnett and Burke Marshall, eds., *Foreign in a Domestic Sense: Puerto Rico, American Expansion, and the Constitution* (Durham: Duke University Press, 2001).
- José Trías Monge, *Puerto Rico: The Trials of the Oldest Colony in the World* (New Haven: Yale University Press, 1997).
- Juan R. Torruella, *The Supreme Court and Puerto Rico: The Doctrine of Separate and Unequal* (San Juan: Editorial de la Universidad de Puerto Rico, 1985).
- Theodore Roosevelt, *Colonial Policies of the United States* (New York: Doubleday, Doran & Company, 1937).


## Legal Article


- Juan R. Torruella, *The Insular Cases: The Establishment of a Regime of Political Apartheid*, 29 University of Pennsylvania Journal of International Law 283 (2007).


## Legal Websites

- The Legal Information Institute of the Cornell University Law School is a wonderful resource for Federal law and regulations.
  https://www.law.cornell.edu/

- SCOTUSBlog is the premier site of analysis on the Supreme Court of the U.S.
  http://www.scotusblog.com/
- Justia provides information on laws and cases, as well as directories for legal blogs and law schools. Old cases of the Supreme Court of the U.S. are available in this site.
  https://www.justia.com/
- The U.S. Congress website has two documents available on the U.S. legislative process:
  - How Our Laws Are Made
    http://www.gpo.gov/fdsys/pkg
    /CDOC-110hdoc49/pdf/CDOC-110hdoc49.pdf
  - Enactment of a Law
    https://www.congress.gov/resources/download
    /attachments/19267597/enactlaw.pdf?version=
    4&modificationDate=1446663432000&api=v2
- *La Oficina de Servicios Legislativos* provides information on the legislative process, as well as the text of laws and resolutions approved by the Puerto Rico Legislative Assembly.
  http://www.oslpr.org/v2/

# Notes

## PREFACE

[1] *Treaty of Peace*, Art. IX.

## CHAPTER 1

[1] *PROMESA*, Discussion Draft, 29 March 2016, 4:08 p.m.

[2] *PROMESA*, Discussion Draft, 24 March 2016, 12:35 p.m.

[3] *PROMESA*, Committee Legislative Summary, 29 March 2016, 1.

[4] *Puerto Rico Chapter 9 Uniformity Act of 2015: Hearing on H.R. 870*, Testimony of Thomas Moers Mayer, 3.

[5] *PROMESA*, Committee Legislative Summary, 29 March 2016, 1.

[6] *PROMESA*, Committee Legislative Summary, 29 March 2016, 1.

[7] *An Act Temporarily to provide revenues and a civil government for Porto Rico [sic], and for other purposes.*

[8] *PROMESA*, Discussion Draft, 24 March 2016, 12:35 p.m., Section 101.

[9] *PROMESA*, Discussion Draft, 29 March 2016, 4:08 p.m., Section 101(c)(1).

[10] *PROMESA*, Discussion Draft, 29 March 2016, 4:08 p.m., Section 101(c)(4).

[11] *PROMESA*, Discussion Draft, 29 March 2016, 4:08 p.m., Section 104(h).

[12] *PROMESA*, Discussion Draft, 24 March 2016, 12:35 p.m., Section 104(j)(1).

[13] *PROMESA*, Discussion Draft, 24 March 2016, 12:35 p.m., Section 110.

[14] *PROMESA*, Discussion Draft, 29 March 2016, 4:08 p.m., Section 107(a)(2).

[15] *PROMESA*, Discussion Draft, 29 March 2016, 4:08 p.m., Section 107(a)(2).

[16] *Federal Labor Standards Act of 1938*, Section 6(g), 29 U.S.C. 206(g).

[17] *PROMESA*, Discussion Draft, 29 March 2016, 4:08 p.m., Section 409.

[18] U.S. Department of Labor, *Defining and Delimiting the Exemptions for Executive, Administrative, Professional, Outside Sales and Computer Employees.*

[19] *PROMESA*, Discussion Draft, 29 March 2016, 4:08 p.m., Section 410.

[20] *PROMESA*, Discussion Draft, 29 March 2016, 4:08 p.m., Section 408.

## CHAPTER 2

[1] *An Act Temporarily to provide revenues and a civil government for Porto Rico [sic], and for other purposes.*

[2] *PROMESA*, Committee Legislative Summary, 29 March 2016, 1.

[3] *PROMESA*, Committee Legislative Summary, 29 March 2016, 1.

[4] Wuestewald, "The Long, Expensive History of Defense Rip-Offs."

[5] *PROMESA*, Discussion Draft, 24 March 2016, 12:35 p.m., Section 201(b)(5).

[6] *PROMESA*, Discussion Draft, 29 March 2016, 4:08 p.m., Section 207(a).

## CHAPTER 3

[1] *PROMESA*, Discussion Draft, 29 March 2016, 4:08 p.m., Section 204(a)(3)(B)(iii).

[2] *PROMESA*, Discussion Draft, 29 March 2016, 4:08 p.m.,

Section 104(h).

[3] *PROMESA*, Discussion Draft, 29 March 2016, 4:08 p.m., Section 208(a).

[4] *PROMESA*, Discussion Draft, 29 March 2016, 4:08 p.m., Section 221(a)(3).

[5] *PROMESA*, Committee Legislative Summary, 29 March 2016, 1.

[6] Aleinikoff, *Semblances of Sovereignty*, 81.

[7] *PROMESA*, Discussion Draft, 29 March 2016, 4:08 p.m., Section 404(2).

[8] *An Act Temporarily to provide revenues and a civil government for Porto Rico [sic], and for other purposes.*

[9] Trigo, "The DoD."

## CHAPTER 4

[1] Casey, "Stay On Litigation."

[2] *PROMESA*, Discussion Draft, 24 March 2016, 12:35 p.m., Section 203(a).

[3] Puerto Rico, *Public Corporation Debt Enforcement and Recovery Act*.

[4] *PROMESA*, Discussion Draft, 29 March 2016, 4:08 p.m., Section 401(1).

## CHAPTER 5

[1] *PROMESA*, Committee Legislative Summary, 29 March 2016, 1.

[2] *PROMESA*, Discussion Draft, 29 March 2016, 4:08 p.m., Section 104(d).

[3] *PROMESA*, Discussion Draft, 29 March 2016, 4:08 p.m., Section 104(d).

[4] Puerto Rico, *Act 76-2000*.

[5] *PROMESA*, Discussion Draft, 29 March 2016, 4:08 p.m.,

Section 501(4).

[6] Trigo, "Crisis and Status."

[7] *PROMESA*, Discussion Draft, 29 March 2016, 4:08 p.m., Section 501(3).

[8] Puerto Rico, *Act 76-2000*, Section 1(a).

[9] Puerto Rico, *Act 76-2000*, Section 2.

[10] Puerto Rico, *Act 76-2000*, Section 2.

[11] *PROMESA*, Discussion Draft, 29 March 2016, 4:08 p.m., Section 501(5).

[12] Puerto Rico, *Public-Private Partnership Act.*

[13] *PROMESA*, Discussion Draft, 29 March 2016, 4:08 p.m., Section 507.

[14] *PROMESA*, Discussion Draft, 29 March 2016, 4:08 p.m., Section 506(c).

## CHAPTER 6

[1] *PROMESA*, H.R. 4900.

[2] *PROMESA*, H.R. 4900, Section 406(m)(5).

[3] *PROMESA*, H.R. 4900 Summary.

[4] *PROMESA*, H.R. 4900 press release, 12 April 2016.

[5] *PROMESA*, H.R. 4900 press release, 13 April 2016.

[6] *PROMESA*, H.R. 4900 Summary.

[7] U.S. House, Committee of Natural Resources, *Puerto Rico Legislation website.*

[8] *PROMESA*, H.R. 4900 How Did We Get Here?

[9] Trigo, "Crisis and Status."

[10] *PROMESA*, H.R. 4900, Section 109.

[11] *PROMESA*, H.R. 4900, Section 104(h).

[12] *PROMESA*, H.R. 4900, Section 204(b)(3).

[13] *PROMESA*, H.R. 4900, Section 201(b)(1).

## CHAPTER 7

[1] *PROMESA*, H.R. 4900, Section 503(a)(1)(E)(vi).

[2] *Consolidated and Further Continuing Appropriations Act of 2015.*

[3] *Consolidated and Further Continuing Appropriations Act of 2015*, Section 9(b).

[4] *Consolidated and Further Continuing Appropriations Act of 2015*, Section 9(d).

[5] *PROMESA*, H.R. 4900, Section 406(l)(4).

[6] *PROMESA*, H.R. 4900, Section 406(m)(5).

[7] Puerto Rico, Senado, *Informe Final*, Resolución del Senado Núm. 237, 78.

## CHAPTER 8

[1] *U.S. v Security Indus. Bank*, 74.

[2] Rogers, *Impairment*, 1017.

[3] *Puerto Rico Chapter 9 Uniformity Act of 2015: Hearing on H.R. 870.*

[4] *Puerto Rico Chapter 9 Uniformity Act of 2015: Hearing on H.R. 870*, Testimony of Thomas Moers Mayer, 3.

[5] *Treaty of Peace.*

[6] In Chapter 21 I suggest books that explain very well these legal decisions and their historical aftermath. If you will be starting to read about these issues, I recommend you start with Bartholomew H. Sparrow's book. Your second reading could be José Trías Monge's book, which has more background on Puerto Rico's history and information on the effects the U.S.'s control has had on Puerto Rico's economic and political development.

## CHAPTER 9

[1] *PROMESA*, H.R. 5278.

[2] *PROMESA*, H.R. 5278 Summary.

[3] *PROMESA,* H.R. 5278 Overview.

[4] *PROMESA,* H.R. 5278 Summary, 1.

[5] *PROMESA,* H.R. 5278 Summary, 1.

[6] Trigo, "The DoD."

[7] *Act to provide for the organization of a Constitutional Government.*

[8] *Approving the Constitution.*

[9] *PROMESA,* H.R. 5278 Summary, 7.

[10] *PROMESA,* H.R. 5278 Summary, 8.

## CHAPTER 10

[1] *PROMESA,* H.R. 5278, Section 408.

[2] U.S. Small Business Administration, *Understanding the HUBZone Program website.*

[3] *PROMESA,* H.R. 5278, Section 101(a).

[4] *PROMESA,* H.R. 5278, Section 409(f).

[5] *PROMESA,* H.R. 5278, Section 404(b).

[6] *An Act Temporarily to provide revenues and a civil government for Porto Rico [sic], and for other purposes,* Section 8; *An Act To provide a civil government for Porto Rico [sic], and for other purposes,* Section 9.

## CHAPTER 11

[1] *PROMESA,* H.R. 5278, Section 104(m).

[2] *PROMESA,* H.R. 5278, Section 108(a)(2).

[3] *PROMESA,* H.R. 4900, Section 108(a)(2).

[4] *PROMESA,* H.R. 5278, Section 107(b).

[5] *PROMESA,* H.R. 5278, Section 204(c)(3).

[6] *PROMESA,* H.R. 5278, Section 201(b)(1)(K).

[7] *PROMESA,* H.R. 4900, Section 201(b)(1)(K).

## CHAPTER 12

[1] *PROMESA,* H.R. 5278, Section 502(b)(2)(A).

## CHAPTER 13

[1] *PROMESA*, H.R. 5278, Section 206(a)(2)(B).

[2] *PROMESA*, H.R. 5278, Section 305(a).

[3] Jacoby, "Presiding Judges."

[4] *PROMESA*, H.R. 5278, Section 314(b)(6).

[5] *PROMESA*, H.R. 5278, Section 602.

[6] *PROMESA*, H.R. 5278, Section 105.

## CHAPTER 14

[1] U.S. House, Committee of Natural Resources, *Markup Hearing for H.R. 5278*, 24 May 2016.

[2] U.S. House, Committee of Natural Resources, *Markup Hearing for H.R. 5278*, 25 May 2016.

[3] U.S. House, Committee of Natural Resources, *Markup Hearing for H.R. 5278*, 25 May 2016, Representative Graves of Louisiana, amendment 1.

[4] U.S. House, Committee of Natural Resources, *Markup Hearing for H.R. 5278*, 25 May 2016, Representative Graves of Louisiana, amendment 46.

[5] U.S. House, Committee of Natural Resources, *Markup Hearing for H.R. 5278*, 25 May 2016, Representative Polis of Colorado, amendment 173.

[6] U.S. House, Committee of Natural Resources, *Markup Hearing for H.R. 5278*, 25 May 2016, Representative Bishop of Utah, amendment 2.

[7] U.S. House, Committee of Natural Resources, *Markup Hearing for H.R. 5278*, 25 May 2016, Representative Bishop of Utah, amendment 1.

[8] U.S. House, Committee of Natural Resources, *Markup Hearing for H.R. 5278*, 25 May 2016, Representative Gallego of Arizona, amendment 46.

[9] U.S. House, Committee of Natural Resources, *Markup*

*Hearing for H.R. 5278*, 25 May 2016, Representative Gallego of Arizona, amendment 45.

[10] U.S. House, Committee of Natural Resources, *Markup Hearing for H.R. 5278*, 25 May 2016, Representative Hice of Georgia, amendment 22.

[11] U.S. House, Committee of Natural Resources, *Markup Hearing for H.R. 5278*, 25 May 2016, Representative MacArthur of New Jersey, amendment 50 revised.

[12] U.S. House, Committee of Natural Resources, *Markup Hearing for H.R. 5278*, 25 May 2016, Representative Zinke of Montana, amendment 1.

[13] Puerto Rico, Departamento de Salud, Orden Administrativa Núm. 346.

[14] U.S. House, Committee of Natural Resources, *Markup Hearing for H.R. 5278*, 25 May 2016, Representative Graves of Louisiana, amendment 2.

[15] U.S. House, Committee of Natural Resources, *Markup Hearing for H.R. 5278*, 25 May 2016. Recorded Vote # 7.

## CHAPTER 15

[1] U.S. House, Committee of Natural Resources, *Markup Report for H.R. 5278*, 3 June 2016.

[2] U.S. House, Committee of Natural Resources, *Markup Report for H.R. 5278*, 3 June 2016, 42.

[3] U.S. House, Committee of Natural Resources, *Markup Report for H.R. 5278*, 3 June 2016, 43.

[4] U.S. House, Committee of Natural Resources, *Markup Report for H.R. 5278*, 3 June 2016, 44.

[5] U.S. House, Committee of Natural Resources, *Markup Report for H.R. 5278*, 3 June 2016, 45.

[6] U.S. House, Committee of Natural Resources, *Markup Report for H.R. 5278*, 3 June 2016, 46.

[7] U.S. House, Committee of Natural Resources, *Markup Report*

*for H.R. 5278*, 3 June 2016, 45.

[8] U.S. House, Committee of Natural Resources, *Markup Report for H.R. 5278*, 3 June 2016, 49.

[9] U.S. House, Committee of Natural Resources, *Markup Report for H.R. 5278*, 3 June 2016, 53.

[10] U.S. House, Committee of Natural Resources, *Markup Report for H.R. 5278*, 3 June 2016, 53.

[11] U.S. House, Committee of Natural Resources, *Markup Report for H.R. 5278*, 3 June 2016, 111.

[12] U.S. House, Committee of Natural Resources, *Markup Report for H.R. 5278*, 3 June 2016, 111.

[13] U.S. House, Committee of Natural Resources, *Markup Report for H.R. 5278*, 3 June 2016, 118.

[14] U.S. House, Committee of Natural Resources, *Markup Report for H.R. 5278*, 3 June 2016, 114.

[15] U.S. House, Committee of Natural Resources, *Markup Report for H.R. 5278*, 3 June 2016, 119-120.

## CHAPTER 16

[1] Congressional Budget Office, *Cost Estimate for H.R. 5278.*

[2] Congressional Budget Office, *Cost Estimate for H.R. 5278*, 1.

[3] Congressional Budget Office, *Cost Estimate for H.R. 5278*, 6.

[4] Congressional Budget Office, *Cost Estimate for H.R. 5278*, 6.

[5] Congressional Budget Office, *Cost Estimate for H.R. 5278*, 6.

[6] Congressional Budget Office, *Cost Estimate for H.R. 5278*, 6.

[7] Congressional Budget Office, *Cost Estimate for H.R. 5278*, 9.

[8] Congressional Budget Office, *Cost Estimate for H.R. 5278*, 6.

[9] Congressional Budget Office, *Cost Estimate for H.R. 5278*, 4.

[10] Congressional Budget Office, *Cost Estimate for H.R. 5278*, 9.

## CHAPTER 17

[1] U.S. House, Committee on Rules, *Rules Committee Print 114-57.*

[2] U.S. House Report 114-610.

[3] U.S. House, Committee on Rules, *Webpage for H.R. 5278.*

[4] *Puerto Rico v Sánchez Valle.*

[5] *Puerto Rico v Sánchez Valle,* 7-8, 12-17 of slip opinion.

[6] *Puerto Rico v Sánchez Valle,* 16 of slip opinion. ("That makes Congress the original source of power for Puerto Rico's prosecutors—as it is for the Federal Government's. The island's Constitution, significant though it is, does not break the chain.")

[7] U.S. House, *Hearing on H.R. 5278,* Amendment to Rules Committee Print 114-57 Offered by Mr. Bishop of Utah.

[8] Puerto Rico, *Act 40-2016.*

[9] U.S. House, *Hearing on H.R. 5278,* Representative Graves of Louisiana, amendment 62.

[10] U.S. House, *Hearing on H.R. 5278,* Representative Jolly of Florida, amendment 48.

[11] U.S. House, *Hearing on H.R. 5278,* Representative Byrne of Alabama, amendment 41.

[12] U.S. House, *Hearing on H.R. 5278,* Representative Byrne of Alabama, amendment 43.

[13] U.S. House, *Hearing on H.R. 5278,* Representative Duffy of Wisconsin, amendment 109.

[14] U.S. House, *Hearing on H.R. 5278,* Representative Serrano of New York, amendment 45.

[15] Puerto Rico, *Act 97-2015.*

[16] U.S. House, *Roll Call 288.*

[17] 162 *Congressional Record* 91, H3567.

## CHAPTER 18

[1] *PROMESA,* S. 2328.

[2] *Puerto Rico v Franklin California Tax-Free Trust.*

[3] *Puerto Rico v Franklin California Tax-Free Trust,* 12 of slip opinion.

[4] U.S. Senate, *Roll Call* 116.

[5] 162 *Congressional Record* 103, S4565.

[6] 162 *Congressional Record* 105, S4683.

## CHAPTER 19

[1] Congressional Research Service, *The Puerto Rico Oversight, Management, and Economic Stability Act (PROMESA; H.R. 5278, S. 2328).*

[2] Trigo, "The DoD."

[3] Puerto Rico, Senado, *Informe Final,* Resolución del Senado Núm. 237, 78.

[4] *PROMESA,* Section 410(3).

[5] *PROMESA,* H.R. 5278, Section 409(f)(1).

# Bibliography

*Act to provide for the organization of a constitutional government by the people of Puerto Rico*. 64 U.S. Statutes at Large 319 (1950). http://www.legisworks.org/congress/81/publaw-600.pdf. [Commonly known as Public Law 600.]

Aleinikoff, T. Alexander. *Semblances of Sovereignty: The Constitution, the State, and American Citizenship*. Cambridge: Harvard University Press, 2002.

*An Act Temporarily to provide revenues and a civil government for Porto Rico [sic], and for other purposes*. 31 U.S. Statutes at Large 77 (1900). http://legisworks.org/sal/31/stats/STATUTE-31-Pg77.pdf. [Commonly known as the Foraker Act of 1900; also as the Organic Act of 1900.]

*An Act To provide a civil government for Porto Rico [sic], and for other purposes*, 39 U.S. Statutes at Large 951 (1917). http://legisworks.org/sal/39/stats/STATUTE-39-Pg951.pdf. [Commonly known as the Jones Act of 1917, enacted on 2 March 2017. It is also referred to as the Jones-Shafroth Act. This is the law through which the U.S. Congress imposed U.S. citizenship upon Puerto Ricans just one month after the U.S. broke diplomatic relations with Germany on 3 February, and a month before the U.S. Congress declared war on Germany on 6 April during the First World War.]

*Approving the constitution of the Commonwealth of Puerto Rico which was adopted by the people of Puerto Rico on March 3, 1952*. 66 U.S. Statutes at Large 327 (1952). https://www.gpo.gov/fdsys/pkg/STATUTE-66/pdf/STATUTE-66-Pg327.pdf

Casey, Jack. "Stay On Litigation Most Controversial Aspect of Puerto Rico Bill." *The Bond Buyer,* 30 March 2016. http://www.bondbuyer.com/news/washington-budget-finance/stay-on-litigation-most-controversial-aspect-of-puerto-rico-bill-1100148-1.html.

Congressional Budget Office. *Cost Estimate for H.R. 5278 As ordered reported by the House Committee on Natural Resources on May 25, 2016.* 114th Cong., 2nd sess., 3 June 2016. https://www.cbo.gov/publication/51650.

Congressional Research Service, *The Puerto Rico Oversight, Management, and Economic Stability Act (PROMESA; H.R. 5278, S. 2328),* 1 July 2016. https://www.hsdl.org/?view&did=794253.

*Consolidated and Further Continuing Appropriations Act of 2015.* 128 U.S. Statutes at Large 2130 (2015). https://www.gpo.gov/fdsys /pkg/PLAW-113publ235/pdf/PLAW-113publ235.pdf.

*Federal Labor Standards Act of 1938,* 52 U.S. Statutes at Large 1062 (1938). Text of Section 6 codified: https://www.gpo.gov/fdsys/granule/USCODE-2011-title29 /USCODE-2011-title29-chap8-sec206/content-detail.html.

Jacoby, Melissa B. "Puerto Rico: PROMESA and Presiding Judges." *Credit Slips,* 26 May 2016. http://www.creditslips.org/creditslips/2016/05/puerto-rico-presiding-over-promesankruptcy.html.

Puerto Rico. Asamblea Legislativa. Senado. Comisión de Derechos Civiles, Participación Ciudadana y Economía Social, *Informe Final,* Resolución del Senado Núm. 237, 17th assembly, 5th sess., 9 April 2015. http://www.oslpr.org/2013-2016/%7B363DC18E-E860-4EA2-B1B3-B6991C308753%7D.doc.

Puerto Rico. Departamento de Salud, Orden Administrativa Núm. 346, *Para Establecer la Política Pública en torno a la Distribución de Productos Naturales o Suplementos Nutricionales o Suplementos Dietéticos,* 9 February 2016. http://www.salud.gov.pr/Estadisticas-Registros-y-Publicaciones/rdenes Administrativas/346-para establecer la politica publica en torno a la distribucion de productos naturales o suplementos nutricionales.pdf.

Puerto Rico. *Act 76-2000.* 2000 Leyes de Puerto Rico 649, 3 LPRA §§ 1931–1945. English version: http://www.oslpr.org/download/en/2000/0076.pdf.

Puerto Rico. *Act 97-2015.* 2015 Leyes de Puerto Rico 701, 3 LPRA § 283d; 7 LPRA §§ 552, 554, 563, 581, 607g-1–607g-8, 607h, 607i, 2111–2123; 22 LPRA § 152a; 23 LPRA § 104. http://www.oslpr.org/2013-2016/leyes/pdf/ley-97-01-Jul-2015.pdf.

Puerto Rico. *Act 40-2016* enacted on 5 May 2016. 2016 Leyes de Puerto Rico ___, 3 LPRA §§ 9283, 9288; 7 LPRA §§ 559, 611j–611l. http://www.oslpr.org/2013-2016/leyes/pdf/ley-40-05-May-2016.pdf.

Puerto Rico. *Public-Private Partnership Act,* 2009 Leyes de Puerto Rico 242, 27 LPRA §§ 2601–2623. English version: http://www.oslpr.org/download/en/2009/A-0029-2009.pdf.

Puerto Rico. *Public Corporation Debt Enforcement and Recovery Act,* 2014 Leyes de Puerto Rico 632, 13 LPRA §§ 111–113nn. English version starts on page 74: http://www.oslpr.org/2013-2016/leyes/pdf/ley-71-28-Jun-2014.pdf. [Commonly known as the Recovery Act or the Puerto Rico Bankruptcy Law.]

*Puerto Rico Oversight, Management, and Economic Stability Act,* 130 U.S. Statutes at Large 549 (2015). https://www.congress.gov/114/bills/s2328/BILLS-114s2328enr.pdf.

*Puerto Rico v. Franklin California Tax-Free Trust,* 579 U.S. ___ (2016). https://www.supremecourt.gov/opinions/15pdf/15-233_i42j.pdf.

*Puerto Rico v Sánchez Valle,* 579 U.S. ___ (2016). https://www.supremecourt.gov/opinions/15pdf/15-108_k4mp.pdf.

Rogers, James S. *The Impairment of Secured Creditors' Rights in Reorganization: A Study of the Relationship Between the Fifth Amendment and the Bankruptcy Clause,* 96 Harvard Law Review 973 (1983).

*Treaty of Peace between the United States of America and the Kingdom of Spain,* 10 December 1898. 30 U.S. Statutes at Large 1754 (1899). http://avalon.law.yale.edu/19th_century/sp1898.asp.

Trigo, María de los Angeles. "Crisis and Status: Puerto Rico on the Brink." *LinkedIn,* 3 July 2015. https://www.linkedin.com/pulse/crisis-status-puerto-rico-brink-maria-de-los-angeles-trigo.

———. "The DoD Finally Rears its Head: Debt as an Excuse." *LinkedIn,* 3 May 2016. https://www.linkedin.com/pulse/dod-finally-rears-its-head-debt-excuse-maria-de-los-angeles-trigo.

*United States* v *Security Indus. Bank,* 459 U.S. 70 (1982). https://supreme.justia.com/cases/federal/us/459/70/case.html
.

U.S. Congress. House. Judiciary Committee. Subcommittee on Regulatory Reform, Commercial and Antitrust Law. *Puerto Rico Chapter 9 Uniformity Act of 2015: Hearing for H.R. 870.* 114th Cong., 1st sess., 26 February 2015.

http://www.judiciary.house.gov/index.cfm/hearings?ID=809AB2A9-78F5-4FCE-8E6D-955F5B6039DE.

U.S. Congress. House. Judiciary Committee. Subcommittee on Regulatory Reform, Commercial and Antitrust Law. *Puerto Rico Chapter 9 Uniformity Act of* 2015: *Hearing for H.R. 870*, Testimony of Thomas Moers Mayer. 114th Cong., 1st sess., 26 February 2015. https://judiciary.house.gov/wp-content/uploads/2016/02/Thomas-Mayer-Testimony.pdf.

U.S. Congress. House. Committee on Natural Resources. *Puerto Rico Oversight, Management, and Economic Stability Act.* Discussion Draft. 114th Cong., 2nd sess., 24 March 2016, 12:35 p.m. https://morningconsult.com/wp-content/uploads/2016/03/PR-Executive-Summary-and-Discussion-Draft.pdf.

U.S. Congress. House. Committee on Natural Resources. *Puerto Rico Oversight, Management, and Economic Stability Act.* Discussion Draft. 114th Cong., 2nd sess., 29 March 2016, 4:08 p.m. http://naturalresources.house.gov/uploadedfiles/puertorico_discussion_draft.pdf.

U.S. Congress. House. Committee on Natural Resources. *Puerto Rico Oversight, Management, and Economic Stability Act.* Discussion Draft Legislative Summary. 114th Cong., 2nd sess., 29 March 2016. http://naturalresources.house.gov/uploadedfiles/puerto_rico_packet.pdf.

U.S. Congress. House. Committee on Natural Resources. *Puerto Rico Oversight, Management, and Economic Stability Act.* H.R. 4900. 114th Cong., 2nd sess., 12 April 2016. http://naturalresources.house.gov/uploadedfiles/hr_4900_promesa.pdf.

U.S. Congress. House. Committee on Natural Resources. *Puerto Rico Oversight, Management, and Economic Stability Act.* H.R. 4900 Summary. 114th Cong., 2nd sess., 12 April 2016. http://naturalresources.house.gov/uploadedfiles/hr_4900_one_pager.pdf.

U.S. Congress. House. Committee on Natural Resources. *Puerto Rico Oversight, Management, and Economic Stability Act.* H.R. 4900 Press Release. 114th Cong., 2nd sess., 12 April 2016. http://naturalresources.house.gov/newsroom/documentsingle.aspx?DocumentID=400231.

U.S. Congress. House. Committee on Natural Resources. *Puerto Rico Oversight, Management, and Economic Stability Act.* H.R. 4900 Press Release. 114th Cong., 2nd sess., 13 April 2016. http://naturalresources.house.gov/newsroom/documentsingle.aspx?DocumentID=400247.

U.S. Congress. House. Committee on Natural Resources. *Puerto Rico Legislation website.* http://naturalresources.house.gov/issues/issue/?IssueID=118691.

U.S. Congress. House. Committee on Natural Resources. *Puerto Rico Oversight, Management, and Economic Stability Act.* H.R. 4900 How Did We Get Here? 114th Cong., 2nd sess., http://naturalresources.house.gov/UploadedPhotos/MediumResolution/73e63a21-7ac3-4b20-b52f-45271b172bcc.jpg.

U.S. Congress. House. Committee on Natural Resources. *Puerto Rico Oversight, Management, and Economic Stability Act.* H.R. 5278. 114th Cong., 2nd sess., 18 May 2016. http://naturalresources.house.gov/uploadedfiles/promesa_hr_5278.pdf.

U.S. Congress. House. Committee on Natural Resources. *Puerto Rico Oversight, Management, and Economic Stability Act.* H.R. 5278 Summary. 114th Cong., 2nd sess., 18 May 2016. http://naturalresources.house.gov/uploadedfiles/promesa_packet_-_5-18.pdf.

U.S. Congress. House. Committee on Natural Resources. *Puerto Rico Oversight, Management, and Economic Stability Act.* H.R. 5278 An Overview of PROMESA's Major Provisions & Key Refinements. 114th Cong., 2nd sess., 18 May 2016. http://naturalresources.house.gov/uploadedfiles/whats_new_promesa.pdf.

U.S. Congress. House. Committee on Natural Resources. *Puerto Rico Oversight, Management, and Economic Stability Act: Markup Hearing for H.R. 5278.* 114th Cong., 2nd sess., 24 May 2016. http://naturalresources.house.gov/calendar/eventsingle.aspx?EventID=400530.

U.S. Congress. House. Committee on Natural Resources. *Puerto Rico Oversight, Management, and Economic Stability Act: Markup Hearing for H.R. 5278.* 114th Cong., 2nd sess., 25 May 2016. http://naturalresources.house.gov/calendar/eventsingle.aspx?EventID=400529.

U.S. Congress. House. Committee on Natural Resources. *Puerto Rico Oversight, Management, and Economic Stability Act: Markup Hearing for H.R. 5278.* Representative Graves of Louisiana. 114th Cong., 2nd sess., 25 May 2016. Text of amendment: http://naturalresources.house.gov/uploadedfiles/hr_5278_graves_1.pdf.

U.S. Congress. House. Committee on Natural Resources. *Puerto Rico Oversight, Management, and Economic Stability Act:*

*Markup Hearing for H.R.* 5278. Representative Graves of Louisiana. 114th Cong., 2nd sess., 25 May 2016. Text of amendment: http://naturalresources.house.gov/uploadedfiles /hr_5278_graves_046.pdf.

U.S. Congress. House. Committee on Natural Resources. *Puerto Rico Oversight, Management, and Economic Stability Act: Markup Hearing for H.R.* 5278. Representative Polis of Colorado. 114th Cong., 2nd sess., 25 May 2016. Text of amendment: http://naturalresources.house.gov/uploadedfiles /hr_5278_polis_173.pdf.

U.S. Congress. House. Committee on Natural Resources. *Puerto Rico Oversight, Management, and Economic Stability Act: Markup Hearing for H.R.* 5278. Representative Bishop of Utah. 114th Cong., 2nd sess., 25 May 2016. Text of amendment: http://naturalresources.house.gov/uploadedfiles/hr_5278_bis hop_2.pdf.

U.S. Congress. House. Committee on Natural Resources. *Puerto Rico Oversight, Management, and Economic Stability Act: Markup Hearing for H.R.* 5278. Representative Bishop of Utah. 114th Cong., 2nd sess., 25 May 2016. Text of amendment: http://naturalresources.house.gov/uploadedfiles/hr_5278_bis hop_1.pdf.

U.S. Congress. House. Committee on Natural Resources. *Puerto Rico Oversight, Management, and Economic Stability Act: Markup Hearing for H.R.* 5278. Representative Gallego of Arizona. 114th Cong., 2nd sess., 25 May 2016. Text of amendment: http://naturalresources.house.gov/uploadedfiles /hr_5278_gallego_046.pdf.

U.S. Congress. House. Committee on Natural Resources. *Puerto Rico Oversight, Management, and Economic Stability Act: Markup Hearing for H.R.* 5278. Representative Gallego of Arizona. 114th Cong., 2nd sess., 25 May 2016. Text of amendment: http://naturalresources.house.gov/uploadedfiles/hr_5278_gallego_045.pdf.

U.S. Congress. House. Committee on Natural Resources. *Puerto Rico Oversight, Management, and Economic Stability Act: Markup Hearing for H.R.* 5278. Representative Hice of Georgia. 114th Cong., 2nd sess., 25 May 2016. Text of amendment: http://naturalresources.house.gov/uploadedfiles/hr_5278_hice_022.pdf.

U.S. Congress. House. Committee on Natural Resources. *Puerto Rico Oversight, Management, and Economic Stability Act: Markup Hearing for H.R.* 5278. Representative MacArthur of New Jersey. 114th Cong., 2nd sess., 25 May 2016. Text of amendment: http://naturalresources.house.gov/uploadedfiles/hr_5278_macarthur_050revised.pdf.

U.S. Congress. House. Committee on Natural Resources. *Puerto Rico Oversight, Management, and Economic Stability Act: Markup Hearing for H.R.* 5278. Representative Zinke of Montana. 114th Cong., 2nd sess., 25 May 2016. Text of amendment: http://naturalresources.house.gov/uploadedfiles/hr_5278_zinke_1.pdf.

U.S. Congress. House. Committee on Natural Resources. *Puerto Rico Oversight, Management, and Economic Stability Act: Markup Hearing for H.R.* 5278. Representative Graves of Louisiana. 114th Cong., 2nd sess., 25 May 2016. Text of amendment: http://naturalresources.house.gov /uploadedfiles/hr_5278_graves_2.pdf.

U.S. Congress. House. Committee on Natural Resources. *Recorded Vote # 7 Favorably Reporting H.R. 5278*. 114th Cong., 2nd sess., 25 May 2016. http://naturalresources.house.gov /uploadedfiles/rc_vote_7_on_favorably_reporting_hr_5278.pd f.

U.S. Congress. House. Committee on Natural Resources. *Markup Report for H.R. 5278*. House Report 114-602. 114th Cong., 2nd sess., 3 June 2016. https://www.congress.gov/114/crpt/hrpt602 /CRPT-114hrpt602-pt1.pdf.

U.S. Congress. House. Committee on Rules. *Puerto Rico Oversight, Management, and Economic Stability Act*. Rules Committee Print 114-57. 114th Cong., 2nd sess., 3 June 2016. http://docs.house.gov/billsthisweek/20160606/CPRT-114-HPRT-RU00-HR5278.pdf.

U.S. Congress. House. Committee on Rules. *Puerto Rico Oversight, Management, and Economic Stability Act*. House Report 114-610. 114th Cong., 2nd sess., 8 June 2016. https://www.congress.gov /114/crpt/hrpt610/CRPT-114hrpt610.pdf.

U.S. Congress. House. Committee on Rules. *Website for the H.R. 5278*. 114th Cong., 2nd sess. https://rules.house.gov/bill/114/hr-5278.

U.S. Congress. House. *Puerto Rico Oversight, Management, and Economic Stability Act: Hearing for H.R. 5278*. Amendment to Rules Committee Print 114-57 Offered by Mr. Bishop of Utah. 114th Cong., 2nd sess., 9 June 2016. http://amendments-rules.house.gov/amendments/BishopRev468162047344734.pdf.

U.S. Congress. House. *Puerto Rico Oversight, Management, and Economic Stability Act: Hearing for H.R. 5278*. Representative Graves of Louisiana, 114th Cong., 2nd sess., 9 June 2016. Text of amendment: http://amendments-rules.house.gov/amendments/GRAVES_062_xml68161359595959.pdf.

U.S. Congress. House. *Puerto Rico Oversight, Management, and Economic Stability Act: Hearing for H.R. 5278*. Representative Jolly of Florida, 114th Cong., 2nd sess., 9 June 2016. Text of amendment: http://amendments-rules.house.gov/amendments/JOLLY_048_xml66161645424542.pdf.

U.S. Congress. House. *Puerto Rico Oversight, Management, and Economic Stability Act: Hearing for H.R. 5278*. Representative Byrne of Alabama, 114th Cong., 2nd sess., 9 June 2016. Text of amendment: http://amendments-rules.house.gov/amendments/BYRNE_041_xml67161228242824.pdf.

U.S. Congress. House. *Puerto Rico Oversight, Management, and Economic Stability Act: Hearing for H.R. 5278*. Representative Byrne of Alabama, 114th Cong., 2nd sess., 9 June 2016. Text of amendment: http://amendments-rules.house.gov/amendments/BYRNE043xml68161231573157.pdf.

U.S. Congress. House. *Puerto Rico Oversight, Management, and Economic Stability Act: Hearing for H.R. 5278*. Representative Duffy of Wisconsin, 114th Cong., 2nd sess., 9 June 2016. Text of amendment: http://amendments-rules.house.gov/amendments/DUFFY_109_xml6716094709479.pdf.

U.S. Congress. House. *Puerto Rico Oversight, Management, and Economic Stability Act: Hearing for H.R. 5278*. Representative Serrano of New York, 114th Cong., 2nd sess., 9 June 2016. Text of amendment: http://amendments-rules.house.gov/amendments/SERRAN_045_xml6816203407347.pdf.

U.S. Congress. House. *Roll Call 288 on passage of H.R. 5278*. 114th Cong., 2nd sess., 9 June 2016. http://clerk.house.gov/evs/2016/roll288.xml

U.S. Congress. Senate. *Puerto Rico Oversight, Management, and Economic Stability Act*. S. 2328. 114th Cong., 2nd sess. https://www.congress.gov/114/bills/s2328/BILLS-114s2328enr.pdf.

U.S. Congress. Senate. *Roll Call 116 on Motion to Concur to House Amendment to S. 2328*. 114th Cong., 2nd sess., 29 June 2016. http://www.senate.gov/legislative/LIS/roll_call_lists/roll_call_vote_cfm.cfm?congress=114&session=2&vote=00116.

*Congressional Record*. 114th Cong., 2nd sess., Vol. 162 No. 91, H3567. https://www.congress.gov/crec/2016/06/09/CREC-2016-06-09.pdf.

*Congressional Record*. 114th Cong., 2nd sess., Vol. 162 No. 103, S4565. https://www.congress.gov/crec/2016/06/27/CREC-2016-06-27.pdf.

*Congressional Record*. 114th Cong., 2nd sess., Vol. 162 No. 105, S4683. https://www.congress.gov/crec/2016/06/29/CREC-2016-06-29.pdf.

U.S. Department of Labor. *Defining and Delimiting the Exemptions for Executive, Administrative, Professional, Outside Sales and Computer Employees*, 29 C.F.R. § 541 (2016). https://www.ecfr.gov/cgi-bin/text-idx?tpl=/ecfrbrowse/Title29/29cfr541_main_02.tpl.

U.S. Small Business Administration. *Understanding the HUBZone Program website*. https://www.sba.gov/contracting

/government-contracting-programs/hubzone-program/understanding-hubzone-program.

Wuestewald, Eric. "The Long, Expensive History of Defense Rip-Offs." *Mother Jones*, 18 December 2013. http://www.motherjones.com/politics/2013/12/defense-military-waste-cost-timeline.

# About the Author

An attorney and CPA with over 20 years of experience in the public and municipal finance area, she advises financial institutions, investors, law firms, think tanks, and government institutions on Puerto Rico debt's legal and regulatory framework.

Ms Trigo worked for 16 years with the Government Development Bank for Puerto Rico and was Director of the Compliance Department and Acting Deputy Director of the Legal Division.

She has a B.B.A. and a J.D. from the University of Puerto Rico.

If you would like to be notified when the book is updated, or when other books are published, you may want to subscribe to her newsletter at www.mtrigo.com/newsletter.

If you have comments on the book write to the author to promesa@mtrigo.com.

www.ingramcontent.com/pod-product-compliance
Lightning Source LLC
Chambersburg PA
CBHW060342200326
41519CB00011BA/2016
* 9 7 8 0 9 9 9 8 0 8 8 1 8 *